Quarks, Chaos, & Christianity

Other titles by John Polkinghorne:

Quarks, Chaos, & Christianity

.

QUESTIONS TO SCIENCE AND RELIGION

JOHN POLIKINGHORNE

CROSSROAD • NEW YORK

1996
The Crossroad Publishing Company
370 Lexington Avenue, New York, NY 10017

Scriptural quotations from
*The Revised Standard Version
of the Bible* © 1971 and 1952.

© John Polkinghorne 1994

Photoset by Rowland Phototypesetting Ltd,
Bury St Edmunds, Suffolk

Printed in the United States of America.

First published in Great Britain 1994
Triangle
Society for Promoting Christian Knowledge
Holy Trinity Church
Marylebone Road
London NW1 4DU

Library of Congress Cataloging-in-Publication Date

Polkinghorne, J. C., 1930–
  [Quarks, chaos, and Christianity]
  Quarks, chaos & Christianity : questions to science and religion /
by John Polkinghorne.
    p. cm.
  Includes bibliographical references.
  ISBN 0-8245-1521-8 (pbk.)
  1. Religion and science. 2. Physics—Religious aspects—
Christianity. I. Title.
  BL240.2.P5754 1995
  261.5'5—dc20   95-30120
                                              CIP

To
our grandchildren,
Katherine, Edward, Rachel,
William, Elizabeth, Adam, and David.

Contents

ACKNOWLEDGEMENTS

Once again I wish to thank my secretary, Mrs Josephine Brown, for her skill and patience in deciphering my handwriting, and typing drafts of the manuscript. I am also grateful to my wife, Ruth, for help with proof correction and the staff of SPCK for their work in preparing the manuscript for press.

John Polkinghorne
The President's Lodge,
Queens' College,
Cambridge
February 1994

Introduction

As someone who's both a scientist and an Anglican priest, I've been concerned with trying to understand how the scientific and religious views of the world relate to each other. Do we have to choose between them or are they, instead, complementary understandings that, seen together, give us a fuller picture than either on their own would provide? I find the best way to sort out what I really think is to try to write it down. The late Bishop John Robinson once said to me that he couldn't think without a pen in his hand, and I knew exactly what he meant. In consequence, I've written six books on different aspects of this question.

Now I've decided it would be useful to try to provide an overview that surveyed the whole scene, rather than concentrating on this or that particular feature of it, as my earlier books have done. At the same time, it gives me the chance to try to set out the main lines of the argument without having to reproduce all the detailed discussion that I've gone into previously. I do a fair amount of speaking on these issues, and I always greatly enjoy the discussion period that normally follows a lecture. This experience has given me some idea of what the main questions are in people's minds, and what are the most helpful insights to offer them. I actually think that we need both science *and* religion, and that they have many important things to say to each other. I hope this short book may help others to share in such a conversation.

Perhaps I should explain that I'm a 'cradle Christian', having grown up in a Christian home, and having always been a part of the worshipping and believing community. I find orthodox Christian belief to be both surprising and exciting, in the same way that a good scientific theory enlarges one's imagination, and satisfies one's intellectual desire for understanding. I've spent most of my working life as a theoretical physicist, and I didn't leave the subject because I was bored or disillusioned with it, but simply because I felt I'd done my bit for it, and the time had come to do something different. I'm driven by the need to take both science and religion seriously, and I'm sure that they are friends, not foes, in the common quest for knowledge.

Some people may find this last remark surprising, for there's a feeling throughout our society that religious belief is outmoded, or downright impossible, in a scientific age. I don't agree. In fact, I'd go so far as to say that if people in this so-called 'scientific age' knew a bit more about science than many of them actually do, they'd find it easier to share my view. The defence of this claim lies in the pages that follow.

1

Fact or Opinion?

Science is very impressive. We all benefit from its successes. I wouldn't be writing this book if the advances in medicine hadn't provided a means for me to survive a serious illness that struck ten years ago. When my secretary types up my scribblings, she'll use all the electronic wizardry of a sophisticated word processor. We all enjoy, every day of our lives, the new things made possible by the advance of science.

Science also enlightens our minds and enlarges our imaginations. We know that we are the inhabitants of an unremarkable planet, circling an unremarkable star, in a universe that contains at least ten thousand million million million stars. Once this universe looked very different to the way it does today, and it has had a long history, going back fifteen billion years to the fiery explosion of the Big Bang that gave it birth. Science tells us what makes the stars shine, why water is wet, how genetic information is conveyed from one generation to the next. It's a story of astonishing achievement, and perhaps the most impressive thing about it is that we can all agree on the answers. The dust really does settle. Not only does science answer questions, it does so to universal satisfaction.

It would be foolish to deny that there's a striking

1

contrast with religion. We'll not all agree on the answer to the most fundamental religious question of them all: 'Is there a God?' Although the different faiths clearly refer to a common human experience of the spiritual, they seem to say such different things about it. Is the individual human self of unique value and significance (so say Judaism, Christianity and Islam) or is it, in fact, an illusion (so says Buddhism) or is it recycled through reincarnation (so says Hinduism)? Is suffering something to be accepted or avoided? And so on.

The conclusion seems clear. Science is based on facts and leads to real knowledge. Religion is just based on opinion. It may help you or me to live our lives—religion may be 'true for me' or 'true for you'—but it's not just plain 'true', pure and simple. So it may seem, but I believe that such a conclusion would be a fundamental mistake of the most disastrous kind. If I thought it were true, I would not be a religious person. How could something really help one in one's life if it were just a personal illusion? Only the true can be a real basis for living—and facing death.

Two mistakes lead to the false conclusion that science and religion involve the encounter of fact with mere opinion. One is a mistake about science. The other is a mistake about religion. Let's take science first.

Many people's impression of how science progresses is that a prediction is made ('adding factor X will turn the liquid green'), an experiment is performed (it does turn green), and a great new discovery has been made. In actual fact, it is all a good deal more subtle and more interesting than that. In the first case, the facts that concern scientists are already *interpreted* facts. Most of the time you can't see directly what's happening. You have to infer it from the things you can see, and that inference requires the use of theoretical interpretation.

It's quite hard to give an example of this for the non-scientist because modern apparatus is so com-

Figure 1 A simplified picture of what is seen in a bubble chamber

plicated and technical, exactly illustrating my point that you have to know the theory in order to understand the experiment. Rather than a 'gee-whizz' discussion of electronic gadgetry, let me just show you a picture. It's meant to represent a photograph of tracks in a device widely used for many years in my old subject of elementary particle physics (the study of the smallest bits of matter). The apparatus is called a bubble chamber. It contains a liquid that is just about to boil. A particle passing through triggers a chain of little bubbles, which make its path visible. It's a bit like bubbles rising in a glass of beer, and, in fact, the man who invented the device is said to have got the idea while brooding on his lunchtime drink. A photograph of a bubble chamber will show lots of these tracks, a complicated pattern of curls and swirls. Figure 1 is a simplified example of this.

Doubtless we could all painstakingly follow each track and agree what sort of shape it had, but this, by itself, would be of no scientific interest whatsoever. The patterns only become significant when they're interpreted as indicating such-and-such a particle moving with such-and-such a speed and being made to curl round by the strong magnetic field applied to the chamber. *Then* it all becomes meaningful and interesting. I remember once being shown a particular photograph that, when its significance was explained by the experimentalists, turned out to show the existence of an entirely new particle. This was really exciting. Without the interpretation, it was just a mess.

Now, the problem is this. In order to make the

interpretation, you have to know some science already. You can't just stare at the world; you have to view it from a chosen point of view. Choosing the point of view involves an act of intellectual daring in betting that things might be this way. This means that in science, experiment and theory, fact and interpretation, are always mixed up with each other. They're as inseparable as the meaning and the ink that together make up the words of this book. Someone once said that scientists wear 'spectacles behind the eyes'—it's not just *what* they see but the *way* that they see it that counts. In other words, science uses a mixture of fact and opinion. Of course there are reasons for the opinions, and opinions can be revised when they don't seem to work very well, but you can't do without them.

There's another reason why this is so that I haven't mentioned so far. In a bubble chamber photograph, there are likely to be some tracks that have nothing to do with the experiment, but are accidental strays, coming, perhaps, from the cosmic rays that continually bombard the Earth from outer space (in my figure, this is probably what the horizontal lines are, the really significant bit being the V at the bottom). In order to interpret what is happening correctly, it is necessary to identify and eliminate these spurious contributions. In the trade, this is called the problem of the 'background'. There is no rule book you can consult to tell you how to strain out these unwanted additional effects. It's a matter of judgement, and so, ultimately, of informed opinion, that this has been accomplished successfully. I could tell you some horror stories of incorrect conclusions that were reached because of errors made about background effects.

The idea that strange effects may be due to unexpected background can also lead to splendid successes. When the planet Uranus was discovered in the eighteenth century, astronomers found that it was not moving through the heavens in the way that Newton's theory of gravity predicted, but his theory was far too beautiful and far too effective to be abandoned without a struggle. Two mathematicians—Adams in England and Leverrier in France—independently hit upon the brilliant idea that the trouble might be due to the unseen presence of yet another planet, beyond Uranus. They were both able to calculate where it should be. I regret to say that the British astronomers were either too lazy or too incredulous to bother to take a look to see if Adams was right, so that the honour of discovering Neptune fell to the French. The moral of this little tale is that trouble in fitting the 'facts' does not instantly disprove a scientific theory. It may just mean that more is going on than we had first appreciated.

The need to mix fact and interpretation, to survey the world from a chosen point of view, makes science more daring, and more precarious than people often realize. Some philosophers have been so struck with this that they've gone on to deny that science can give us any reliable knowledge of how things actually are. Perhaps it's not discovery at all, but just an unconscious agreement among the scientists to see it this way. Of course, such philosophers don't deny that science scores successes in getting things done, but they do suggest that this is all that science is up to—it's a collection of technologically useful manners of speaking. A road map is handy in helping one get from A to B, but we don't believe that motorways are thin blue lines or towns are thick black dots.

But wait a minute! Although a map is not the whole truth about the countryside, unless it represented at least part of the truth, it wouldn't work at all. That's what I believe about science. It never succeeds in telling us the *whole* truth about the physical world—there are always new things to find out—but, surely, it tells us *some* of the truth. We may not know all there is to know about atoms or electrons, but surely there *are* atoms and electrons. Science makes maps of the physical world that are reliable for some, but not every, purpose.

I believe this about science for three reasons. The first is one I've already hinted at. It seems impossible to believe that science could have been as successful as it is unless it really did represent aspects of the way things are. Take the idea of electrons, the smallest particles of matter whose movement makes electric currents flow. We can also use them to understand how chemistry works, to make electron microscopes powerful enough to 'see' atoms, to construct electronic devices of all kinds, and to do many more things besides. How could we manage all this unless there really were electrons with the kinds of properties we've discovered? To most people, this will seem obvious. I think the philosophers should agree with them.

Another reason why we should believe that sci-

7

ence tells us what the world is like, is that it often turns out to be entirely different to what we expected. The physical world imposes itself on us as having its own nature, which we discover but in no way invent. Let me give you an example. One of the questions that perplexed scientists from the earliest days was 'What is the nature of light?' Newton rather cautiously speculated that it might be made of little bullets. His Dutch contemporary, Huyghens, felt that it was more likely to consist of waves. In the nineteenth century, it seemed that the matter had been settled. Thomas Young (who also helped decipher Egyptian hieroglyphics) did some pretty experiments that showed some absolutely typical wave effects. Waves add together in different ways according to whether they are in step or not. If they are, two crests come together and reinforce each other; if they are not, a crest and a trough can coincide and cancel each other out. One effect brightens the light, the other darkens it. Young found that this variation of light and darkness did indeed happen. Later in the century, in one of the most brilliant discoveries of all time in physics, James Clerk Maxwell identified light as waves of electromagnetic energy. The question seemed settled in a most conclusive and satisfactory way. Imagine everyone's astonishment (and unease) when, in the early years of this century, Max Planck and Albert Einstein showed that, in some circumstances, light behaved, not as waves, but as bullets! I'll say some more about this later, but, for the moment, notice two things: first, no one wanted to believe that light was sometimes bullet-like, they were just driven to it by the way things are, and, second, even when we think we understand the physical world pretty well, looking at it more closely may show that it still has surprises in store for us.

My final reason for belief that science is about the way the things are, is that what scientists really want to do is not to get things done by inventing clever devices, but to *understand* what the physical world is actually like. Let me tell you a parable to make the point. One day, a big black box is delivered at the Meteorological Office. With it comes an instruction booklet that reads 'feed in the details of today's weather at slot A, turn the handle, and out from slot B will come a prediction of the weather in a week's time!' It seems pretty unlikely, but they're an open-minded lot at the Met Office and so they give it a go. Lo and behold, it works! Time and again the predictions are found to be correct. If the Met Office is simply about weather forecasting, simply about getting things done, its task is fully accomplished, but do you think those meteorologists would all pack up and go home? Not a bit of it. They don't want just to *predict* the weather, they want to *understand* how it arises from the interaction between the Earth's seas, land masses and atmosphere. Within a few weeks, they would be tampering with the seals on that black box in an endeavour to understand why it was able to model the behaviour of weather systems so perfectly.

You may be feeling a bit impatient. I've spent some pages defending the idea that science tells us what the physical world is like. Most people think this is obvious. I certainly think it's true, but, because science is really rather subtle in the way it works, I don't think it *is* obvious. It was worth looking at the question in detail because science's successful mixture of fact and opinion tells us something about how we get knowledge and this may prove helpful in other spheres as well. It's time to take a look at religion.

Everyone knows that religion involves faith. Many people seem to think that faith involves shutting one's eyes, gritting one's teeth, and believing six impossible things before breakfast, because the Bible or the Pope or some other unquestionable authority tells us so. Not at all! Faith may involve a leap, but it's a leap into the light, not the dark. The aim of the religious quest, like that of the scientific quest, is to seek motivated belief about what is the case. We have already said that religion can only be of real value if it's actually true. It's not a technique for whistling in the dark to keep our spirits up.

When I decided that I'd done my little bit for science, and the time had come for me to do something else (in fact, become a clergyman), I had an interesting period of eighteen months or so in which I was winding up my academic affairs. I couldn't just leave my research students, saying 'Cheerio, I hope you get a Ph.D.'.

During this period I had a number of interesting conversations with my colleagues in the international intellectual 'village' that was the community of theoretical high energy physicists. 'John, what are you up to?', they would say. Usually they were asking the more basic question of why I was a Christian, rather than the vocational question of why I had decided to turn my collar around. Over a cup of coffee in some laboratory canteen, I would try to explain my Christian belief. I knew that I had to do so by appealing to evidence. 'What makes you think this might be true?' was the question to which I had to reply. In a half-hour conversation, it was scarcely possible to do more than make a few simple points (I'd have been similarly constrained if I'd been trying to convey to a non-scientist the reasons for my belief in quarks and gluons as constituents of matter). There was quite a complicated structure of interlocking experience and insight that had to be gone over in order to give a full explanation. In the end, I wrote a little book with a grandiose title, *The Way the World Is* (Triangle, 1983), setting out the reasons for my Christian faith as I would have done if I'd had several hours at my disposal to tell the story.

I don't want to repeat this exercise here. All I want to do is emphasize that there was a whole string of evidential questions to be addressed. How reliable is the New Testament? What can we actually know about Jesus? Are there reasons for believing the claims that he was raised from the dead? What are we to make of that strange phenomenon, the Christian Church, that has given rise both to St Francis *and* the Inquisition? For faith to be possible, rational responses to these questions are required.

I believe that science and religion are intellectual cousins under the skin. Both are searching for motivated belief. Neither can claim absolutely certain knowledge, for each must base its conclusions on an interplay between interpretation and experience. In consequence, both must be open to the possibility of correction. Neither deals simply with pure fact, or with mere opinion. They are both part of the great human endeavour to *understand*.

Nevertheless, there are obviously differences between science and religion. One of the most significant is that science deals with a physical world that is at our disposal to kick around or pull apart as we please. In short, science can put things to the experimental test. God, however, is not at our disposal in this way. The Bible says, 'You shall not put the Lord your God to the test'. It's no good saying, 'If there is a God, let him strike me down dead'. He just doesn't play that sort of silly game. Nor do people. If I'm always setting little traps to see if you're my friend, in actual fact I'll destroy the possibility of real friendship between us by the distrust I display. In the realm of personal experience, whether between ourselves or with God, we all know that *testing* has to give way to *trusting*.

There are some branches of science that are also impossible to test. Cosmology and evolutionary biology are examples. We don't have a lot of universes on which to try out our ideas; we have to make the best sense we can of the one world whose history is partly known to us. In the same way, we can't rerun the evolution of life to see how things would change if circumstances had been different. In these historical sciences, we just have to find the most satisfactory explanation of the limited, and in some ways fragmentary, evidence at our disposal. These historical sciences are sources of considerable insight nevertheless. They are the closest scientific cousins to theology.

Another difference between scientific knowledge and religious knowledge lies in the consequences that they have for us. My belief in quarks and gluons is intellectually satisfying, but it doesn't affect my life in a radical way. God, on the other hand, is not just there to satisfy our curiosity. The encounter with him will involve the call to obedience as well as the illumination of our minds. Religious knowledge is much more demanding than scientific knowledge. While it requires scrupulous attention to matters of truth, it also calls for the response of commitment to the truth discovered.

If we're really to understand this rich and complicated world in which we live, we shall need the help of all these forms of enquiry. Science, by itself, would be a hopelessly limited and impoverished view of things. Music would just be vibrations in the air. A beautiful painting would just be a collection of specks of paint of known chemical composition. As part of its technique of enquiry, science ignores questions of value, but this doesn't for a moment mean that values don't exist or that they're not of the highest importance. Nearly all that makes life worth living slips through the wide meshes of the scientific net. In my friendly arguments with my unbelieving friends, I'm always trying to encourage them to lift their eyes beyond the limited horizons of the scientific view. I believe that beauty is not mere emotion, and that it provides an important window into the nature of reality. I think that I know, as certainly as I know anything, that torturing children is wrong, and that love is better than hate. I cannot for a moment suppose that these ethical insights are merely cultural choices of the particular society in which I happen to live. One of the attractions of belief in God is that it ties together these very different aspects of the one world of our human experience. The feeling of wonder at the beautiful structure of the physical universe, which is so fundamental an experience for the scientist, and is the reward for all the weary labour involved in scientific research, is a recognition of the mind of the Creator. Our experiences of beauty are a sharing in his joy in creation. Our ethical intuitions are intimations of his good and perfect will. It is not that atheists are stupid, but simply that theism explains more, and is more intellectually satisfying.

Another form of human experience that is made intelligible by belief in God is, of course, religious experience itself. We should remember that almost all people, at all times and in all places, have had some form of religious belief. The widespread unbelief of the contemporary Western world is a limited phenomenon, both historically and geographically. Just as the tone deaf should consider seriously the possibility that those who enjoy music are on to something worth while, so should Western unbelievers consider the possibility that they are missing something vital. I would identify two general characteristics of religious experience. One is worship, the recognition, however fitfully and faintly, of encounter with a Reality who is worthy of awe and honour. The other is hope. Despite all the bitter suffering of the world, there is a deep intuition set in the human heart, that Reality is trustworthy, that the comforting of a disturbed child is not the acting of a loving lie, but the assertion of a true insight.

We need the insights of both science *and* religion in our quest for understanding. Science is essentially asking, and answering, the question 'How?' By what manner of means do things come about? Religion, essentially, is asking and answering the question 'Why?' Is there a meaning and purpose at work behind what is happening? We need to address both these questions if we're to understand what is going on. The kettle is boiling because the gas is burning. The kettle is boiling because I wish to make a cup of tea (and will you have one?) We don't have to choose between these two answers. We need both. However, although the two questions 'How?' and 'Why?' are different, their answers must bear some believable relationship to each other. The statements, 'I have put the kettle in the refrigerator', and 'I intend to make a cup of tea' just don't fit together. Because of this need to make mutual sense, science and religion have things to say to each other.

The rest of this book will be an exploration of what this necessary conversation between science and religion is like. Let me draw a moral from science that can be of help to theology in its search for understanding. I have already referred to the astonishing and perplexing way in which light has been found to behave, that is, sometimes like waves, and sometimes like particles. A wave is a spread-out flappy thing; particles are like little bullets. To our common-sense minds, it seems absurd that the same .entity should behave in such radically different ways, yet no progress would have been made by denying the severity of the problem. It was no use trying to sweep the particle discoveries of Planck and Einstein under the carpet, or trying to forget about the earlier wave discoveries of Young and Clerk Maxwell. It was an apparently ridiculous situation, but people just had to hang on to basic experience by the skin of their intellectual teeth, even if they couldn't make head nor tail of it. I am glad to say that it all had a happy ending. In Cambridge in the late 1920s, Paul Dirac was able to invent something called quantum field theory, which explained how light could give a wave-like answer if you asked a wave-like question, or a particle-like answer if you asked a particle-like question. Nature was not irrational after all, but it had a deeper rationality than we could ever have guessed beforehand.

If science teaches you anything, it is that the world is full of surprises. Common sense is not the measure of everything. Quantum theory tells us that the way things behave on the scale of atoms or smaller is totally different to the way that 'large' objects behave in our everyday world. There is a price to be paid for the clever trick of being able to be sometimes like a wave and sometimes like a particle. The cost is a lack of precise information about what exactly is going on. If you have something like an electron, then, if you know where it is, you can't know what it's doing; if you know what it's doing, you can't know where it is. That's Heisenberg's celebrated Uncertainty Principle in a nutshell. This strange quantum world is unpicturable for us, but, nevertheless, we find that, in the end, we can understand it. We learn to respect its strange ways, and see that they make their own kind of sense.

I hardly need to labour the moral of this for theology. If the unpicturable world of electrons gives us some surprises, we shouldn't be too amazed if the unpicturable God has some surprises in store for us also. If, as a Christian believer, I find—as I do, and as millions have done before me—that when I talk of Jesus Christ I can't just talk about him in human terms, but I'm also driven to use divine language, then I have to accept the reality of this experience, however difficult it is to understand how the infinite God and a finite man in first-century Palestine can, in some mysterious way, be joined together.

I'm not saying anything as ridiculous as, 'Quantum theory is odd, so after it anything goes'. I *am* saying 'We cannot decide beforehand what the nature of reality (whether God or the physical world) is going to turn out to be'. This can only be discovered by submitting ourselves to actual experience. So, you see, it's not a case of scientific fact versus religious opinion. It's a case, with both science and religion, of trying to interpret and understand the rich, varied, and surprising way the world actually is.

Let me end this chapter by suggesting that religion has done something for science. The latter came to full flower in its modern form in seventeenth-century Europe. Have you ever wondered why that's so? After all, the ancient Greeks were

pretty clever and the Chinese achieved a sophisticated culture well before we Europeans did, yet they
didn't hit on science as we now understand it. Quite
a lot of people have thought that the missing ingredient was provided by the Christian religion. Of
course, it's impossible to prove that this is so—we
can't rerun history without Christianity and see
what happens—but there's a respectable case worth
considering. It runs like this.

The way Christians think about creation (and the
same is true for Jews and Moslems) has four significant consequences. The first is that we expect the
world to be orderly, because its Creator is rational
and consistent, yet he is also free to create a universe
whichever way he chooses. Therefore, we can't
figure it out just by thinking what the order of
nature ought to be, we'll have to take a look and
see. In other words, observation and experiment are
indispensable. That's the bit the Greeks missed.
They thought you could do it all just by cogitating.
Third, because the world is God's creation, it's
worthy of study. Fourth, because the creation is not
itself divine, we can prod it and investigate it without impiety. Put all these features together, and you
have the intellectual setting in which science can get
going.

It's certainly a historical fact that most of the pion-
eers of modern science were religious men. They
may have had their difficulties with the Church (like
Galileo) or been of an unorthodox cast of mind (like
Newton), but religion was important for them.
They used to like to say that God had written two
books for our instruction, the book of scripture and

the book of nature. I think we need to try to decipher both books if we're to understand what's really happening.

2

Is There Anyone There?

If there is a God, one might expect that he would give us some clues to the fact of his existence. These might be of two kinds. One sort would be through particular moments in history, or particular people, by means of which the divine purpose was made especially clear. All the great religions look to foundational events and people in this kind of way, as sources of revelation about God. Judaism looks to Moses and the deliverance of Israel from slavery in Egypt; Christianity to Jesus Christ, his death, and resurrection; Islam to the prophet Mohammed and the dictation of the Qur'ān; and so on. As science is concerned with what happens in general, it does not have much to say about such particular happenings, which slip through its impersonal net. The scientific habit of thought—of looking for evidence to back up claims for significance—can be helpful in approaching these matters, but it will have to be tailored to the unique character of the events involved. We've already noted that religion is about the personal, which means the individual and unrepeatable.

There's a second way that God might be glimpsed—through the character of the world he's claimed to have made. We wouldn't expect it to be full of objects stamped 'Made by God'—he's more subtle than that—but we would anticipate that there'd be some clues to its being his creation. Here science *can* be expected to help. If there's a purpose behind what's going on, the way science answers its 'How?' questions should encourage us to go on to ask the religious question 'Why?' as well. Of course, it won't be a direct connection. We mustn't confuse science with religion, but some sort of nudge in a religious direction seems a reasonable thing to look for if there really is a God behind the scenes of the universe.

But wait a minute! Haven't we been here before? From the seventeenth century onwards, people used to write books saying how wonderfully adapted life is to its environment. One has only to think of the marvellously efficient optical system of the human eye to get the point. Didn't such signs of design point one inevitably to the presence of a Designer? It all sounded pretty convincing, until Darwin drew the rug from beneath such authors' feet by showing how his theory of evolution could account for apparent design *without* the intervention of a divine Designer. The patient accumulation and sifting of small differences through generations of natural selection would automatically do the trick. At a blow, religion lost one of its most powerful natural arguments.

So, am I going to make the same mistake all over again? I think not. The trouble with the old arguments was that they were trying to give theological answers to what were actually scientific questions. We've learned that these scientific questions can be expected to receive scientific answers. Science can get

21

on with its own task without needing a kind of spurious help from religion. To claim otherwise would be to make the mistake of the God of the gaps, where he popped up as the 'explanation' of what was currently scientifically unknown. The trouble was that, like the Cheshire Cat, he tended to fade away. The advance of knowledge made him redundant. We've learned not to make rash statements like, 'Only God's direct action could bring life out of inanimate matter!' In fact, we don't yet understand scientifically how life arose, but we've no reason to think that one day we won't find out.

The God of the gaps was actually a *theological* mistake. If God's the Creator, he's somehow connected with the whole show, not just the difficult or murky bits of what's going on. What form this Creatorly connection takes is something I'll discuss in the next chapter. For the moment, let's go back to considering whether or not the universe shows any signs of actually being a creation.

I suppose it comes down to asking whether or not there's more worth telling than the scientific story alone. Are we simply content with what science can say to us? I think we shouldn't be, and, interestingly, this is partly because science itself throws up some questions from its own experience that go beyond its own power to answer. In other words, there are aspects of nature that science has to take for granted, but which, it seems to me, *we* shouldn't take for granted. We should try to understand why they are the way they are. They centre on two big questions: 'Why can we do science at all?' and 'Why is the universe so special?'

We're so used to using science to understand the world that we seldom stop to think how odd it is that this is possible. Of course, we must have an everyday understanding of everyday things, otherwise we wouldn't be able to keep alive at all. We'd soon come to grief if we didn't know that there's something pulling us down to earth, so that it's a bad idea to step off a high ladder. However, to be able to go on beyond this; and to understand with Newton that it is the same gravitational force that also keeps the Moon circling the Earth and the Earth circling the Sun; and then with Einstein to realize that this is due to the curvature of space-time (that is, that mass and energy actually bend space and time); and that it explains the structure of the whole universe—this is an ability that goes far beyond anything we need for survival. Where do we get this marvellous power to understand things?

Actually, it's even odder than this, for it's *mathematics* that confers this strange ability. I suppose one of the greatest scientists I've ever known was Paul Dirac, who, for more than thirty years, occupied Newton's old professorship in Cambridge. He was one of the founding fathers of quantum theory, and he spent his life looking for beautiful equations. You might find this a rather odd idea, but mathematical beauty is something that those with an eye for such matters can recognize quite easily. Dirac looked for beautiful equations because, time and again, we've found that they're the ones that describe the physical world. Dirac once said that it was more important to have beauty in your equations than to have them agree with experiment! Of course, he didn't mean that it didn't matter whether or not the equations fitted the facts, but if there was a discrepancy it might be due to not solving the equations correctly, or, even, that the experiments might be wrong. At least, there was a chance that it would all work out in the end, but, if the equations were ugly . . . , well, then there was no chance at all.

When we use mathematics in this way—as the key to unlocking the secrets of the universe—something very strange is happening. Mathematics is pure thought. Our mathematical friends sit in their studies and they dream up, out of their heads, the beautiful patterns of pure mathematics (that's what mathematics is really about, making and analyzing patterns). What I'm saying is that some of the most beautiful of these patterns are actually found to occur, out there, in the structure of the physical world around us. So, what ties together the reason within (the mathematics in our heads), and the reason without (the structure of the physical world)? Remember, it's a very deep connection, going far beyond anything we need for everyday survival. Why is the world so *understandable*?

This puzzled Einstein. He once said that the only incomprehensible thing about the universe is that it's comprehensible. Why can we figure it out so well? Why is science possible?

You have a choice. You can always shrug your shoulders and say 'That's just the way it is, and a bit of luck for you chaps who are good at maths'. This, it seems to me, is just incredibly lazy. My instinct, as a scientist, is to try to understand things as thoroughly as possible. I can't give up a lifetime's habit just at this point. You could think about it in the following way. What I've been saying is that the universe, in its rational beauty and transparency, looks like a world shot through with signs of mind, and, maybe, it's the 'capital M' Mind of God we are seeing. In other words, the reason within and the reason without fit together because they have a common origin in the reason of the Creator, who is the ground of all that is. An ancient verse in Genesis comes to mind, which says that humanity is made 'in the image of God'. I actually think this is what makes science possible.

It's important to be clear about what I'm claiming. I'm not saying, 'Science works, therefore God exists, QED'. In actual fact, I don't think one can *prove* either that God exists or that he doesn't exist— we're in an area of discussion that is too deep for mere proof. I *am* saying, that the existence of the Creator would explain why the world is so profoundly intelligible, and I can't see any other explanation that works half as well.

A big, fundamental question, like belief in God (or disbelief), is not settled by a single argument. It's too complicated for that. What one has to do is to consider lots of different issues and see whether or not the answers one gets add up to a total picture that makes sense. For me, our power to understand the physical world is just one part of a total case for religious belief.

Another part of the same case comes from realizing that we live in a universe that is incredibly special, and that the only reason we're here at all is because this is so. It isn't the case that evolution by itself is enough to explain our origins. Almost all universes we can think of would be sterile, incapable of evolving life however long you waited for them to do so. This is such an important and surprising conclusion that it's given its own learned name, The Anthropic Principle (deriving from *anthropoi*, the Greek word for humankind).

Let me put it this way. Suppose God were to lend you the use of his Universe–Creating Machine. As you approached this no doubt impressive piece of machinery, you would find that there were a large number of knobs for you to adjust. They would specify the scientific structure of the world you were going to create. For example, there would be a set of knobs relating to gravity. One would be an on/off switch: do you want gravity in your world at all, and, if you do, what kind? Inverse square law (like Newton discovered in our universe) or some other form? Once you've decided this, there's another knob to adjust to determine how strong you want gravity to be. It may surprise you to learn that, in the way scientists measure these things, gravity is actually a very weak force in our world (it may not seem so if you've ever fallen out of an upstairs window, but this is due to the fact that gravity always adds up; nothing cancels it out). Perhaps you'd like it stronger in your universe, or even weaker? You decide, and twiddle the knobs accordingly. Then, all the other forces of nature await your attention. There's electromagnetism, the force that holds matter (and us) together. In our universe it's much stronger than gravity. How would you like it to be in yours? So it would be for the other forces of nature. Finally, there are some knobs to determine size and such-like qualities. Do you want a vast universe, like ours with its trillions of stars, or something a bit smaller and more domestic?

Right! All the knobs are set, you pull the handle and out comes the universe God has allowed you to create. You wait to see what happens. You'll have to be patient, it may take billions of years. I suppose my guess would be that, in the end, most universes would do something interesting if you waited long enough. Changing the forces would have some effects. For example, if you made gravity stronger, 'people' would be shorter because it would be harder to grow tall. Whatever happened, some sort of fruitful outcome would surely result. Not necessarily human beings, of course, but perhaps little green men. I would have been completely wrong!

We now understand that unless you had set these knobs very precisely, finely tuned them to specifications extremely close to those of our own universe, the world you had decided to create would have had a dull and sterile history. It would not have produced anything like such interesting consequences as you and me. We live in a very special universe—one in a trillion you might say.

This is a very surprising conclusion and I'd like to sketch some of the reasons we have for reaching it. First, you've got to be careful to get off to a good start. If your universe expands too quickly from its initial Big Bang, it will rapidly become too dilute for anything interesting to happen in it. On the other hand, if it expands too slowly, it will recollapse before anything interesting happens. Your universe had also better be pretty smooth, otherwise large irregularities in its early history will generate catastrophically destructive turbulence. However, it mustn't be absolutely smooth either as, if there is no grainyness at all, then stars and galaxies will be unable to form.

You need stars because they have two absolutely indispensable roles to play in making life possible. One role, of course, is as reliable sources of energy. Life has been able to evolve on Earth because the Sun has been a steadily burning source of energy for the billions of years during which evolution has been happening. We know what makes stars burn uniformly for very long periods: it is a delicate balance between gravity and electromagnetism. Disturb this balance, and stars either become too cool to act as effective energy sources, or so hot that they burn away in a matter of a mere few million years—far too short a time to bring about life. So, you had better set those gravity and electromagnetic control knobs pretty carefully.

However, this won't be enough by itself, for stars have a second vital role to play. They are the nuclear furnaces in which are made the elements that are the raw materials of life. For the first three minutes of its history, the whole universe was hot enough to be the arena of nuclear reactions. It was like a cosmic hydrogen bomb. However, the very early universe was also very simple, and so it could only do very simple things. It made only the two simplest elements, hydrogen and helium. They don't have an interesting enough chemistry to provide the basis for life. For this you need the richer possibilities provided by the heavier elements. In particular, you need the very fertile chemistry of carbon. Every atom of carbon inside our bodies was once inside a star. We are all made from the ashes of dead stars.

To make carbon in a star, three helium nuclei have to be made to stick together. This is tricky to achieve and only possible because a special effect (technically, a resonance) is present in just the right place. This delicate positioning depends upon the strong nuclear force that holds nuclei together. Change this force a little, and you loose the resonant effect. Also, carbon is not enough; for life one needs lots more elements. Oxygen, for instance. You make it by sticking another helium nucleus on to a carbon one. This must be possible to do, but not too readily, otherwise all your hard-won carbon will turn into oxygen and you've lost it. This is another constraint on the nuclear forces. This delicately balanced chain of nuclear reactions can continue, if the knobs are set just right, up to iron. Inside a star, you can't get any further than this for iron is the most stable nucleus and it won't easily change into anything bigger. So, two tasks remain. One is to make the elements beyond iron, some of which, like zinc and iodine, are essential for life. The other is to ensure that the elements you've already made are actually available for the coming-into-being of life. There's no point in their being locked up, useless, inside the cooling core of a dying star. So, some stars will have to explode as supernovae, scattering their life-generating elements into space, where they can form the chemical environment of second-generation stars and planets as these condense out of the debris of the explosion. If we're made of star-dust, there must be some dust from stars around. If you're very clever, you can adjust the knobs so that the heavier elements (zinc, iodine, and so on) are made in the course of these supernovae explosions. Doing this places a tight constraint on the weak nuclear force, responsible for certain types of radioactive decay.

You may not have followed all the details of the foregoing discussion, but I'm sure you will see that making the raw materials for life is no trivial matter. It is only possible at all in a very special universe. I could go on giving examples of these necessary 'fine tunings', and, in fact, people write whole books detailing the considerations that make up the Anthropic Principle. Let me be content with just one more example, this time relating to the knob marked 'size'.

When we think of our universe with its trillions upon trillions of stars, we can easily get upset about our apparent insignificance as inhabitants of what is, effectively, just a speck of cosmic dust. We should not, though, because, if all those stars were not there, we wouldn't be here to be daunted by the thought of them. It would be no use adjusting the size knob to produce a world much smaller than the one in which we live. This is because modern cosmology recognizes that there is a correlation between how big a universe is and how long its history will last. Only a cosmos at least as big as ours could endure for the fifteen billion years necessary for evolving carbon-based life. You need ten billion years for the first-generation stars to make the carbon, then about five billion years for evolution to yield beings of our sort of complexity. It's a process that just can't be hurried.

Now, what are we to make of all this? First, we must consider some scientific points. Maybe some of these apparently remarkable coincidences are actually just straightforward consequences of a deeper underlying theory, and so don't require 'fine tuning' at all. In fact, scientists have already recognized an example of this possibility. The necessary conditions in the very early universe—just the right rate of expansion, and the right degree of smoothness—probably don't have to be written in, but are achieved automatically by a physical process called 'inflation', which many think took place when the universe was a minute fraction of a second old. It's a kind of 'boiling' of space, and, although it's a guess that this happened, in my view, it's a pretty plausible guess. This doesn't mean that it would happen in just any old universe, though. Once again, it's only a very *particular* kind of universe that could boil up in this sort of way. So, I think that, although there may be other explanatory insights to come, it will still be the case that a world capable of evolving carbon-based life is a very special kind of universe.

However, maybe this is where we've smuggled something in. The Anthropic Principle might really more properly be called the Carbon Principle, for most of its considerations are directed towards the conditions necessary for the evolution of carbon-based life. Perhaps this just shows a lack of imagination. Perhaps other universes have their own forms of intelligent 'conscious life', but are totally different to the way things are in our world. They are fruitful in *their* way, not ours. This is an awfully difficult argument to respond to, because those who make such a claim are drawing very large intellectual blank cheques on a totally unknown account. All I can say is that consciousness seems to demand very great physical complexity to sustain it (our brains are incomparably the most complicated physical systems we have ever encountered, anywhere), and it is far from persuasive that there are many alternative routes to the generation of such complexity.

So, I conclude that it is right to take seriously the insight that a universe capable of evolving beings roughly of our complexity, is a very special universe indeed. Once again, we face a choice. Are we on to something, or do we just shrug our shoulders and say, 'We're here because we're here and that's that'? Once again, I can't be as intellectually lazy as that. At this stage, someone may protest that surely one can't learn much from one example, and we only have one universe to think about. I think this protest is misconceived. While we only have direct scientific experience of one universe, we can certainly *imagine* a whole portfolio of different worlds. Indeed, the last few pages have been just such an exercise. When we do so, we see that our universe has this special quality of 'fine tuning' for life. This strongly suggests to me that there is something interesting in the Anthropic Principle that we should seek to understand.

John Leslie is a philosopher who shares my view. He does a lot of his philosophizing in the beguiling style of telling stories. In his book *Universes* (Rout-ledge, 1989), he tells the following tale. You are about to be executed. You are tied to the stake and your eyes are bandaged. Ten highly trained marks-men have their rifles levelled at your chest. The officer gives the command to fire and the shots ring out . . . You find you have survived! What do you do, just shrug your shoulders and say 'Well, here we are then, that was a close one'? Of course not. You will want to understand what was happening, why you didn't die. Leslie suggests that there are only two rational explanations of your good for-tune. One is that many, many executions are taking place today and you just happen to be in the one in which they all miss. The other explanation is that more was going on than you had realized; the firing party was on your side.

You will see how this translates into thinking about a finely tuned, anthropically fruitful, universe. *Some* explanation is necessary.

One possibility is that there are many, many uni-verses, each with its own natural laws and circum-stances. In other words, those 'imaginary' universes we thought about are real after all, but separate from our world. If there is a vast number of them, then, by chance, in one of them, the conditions will be right for the evolution of life—and, of course, it's the one we live in because we couldn't appear in any other.

The other explanation is that there is only *one* universe, but more is going on in it than we had realized. In other words, it's not just 'any old world', but it's special and finely tuned for life because it is the creation of a Creator who wills that should be so.

Notice that *both* explanations go beyond what science itself can tell us. Scientifically, we have no reason to believe in the existence of any other universe than our own (people sometimes pretend that it is not the case for the many universes explanation, but, believe me, it is, if we are careful and scrupulous about what science can actually say). Leslie says that, simply in relation to the significance of fine tuning, either explanation is equally plausible. I think this is right, but, of course, I believe there are other reasons for believing in God and so, for me, creation is far the better understanding.

Asking and answering the questions, 'Why can we do science at all?', and 'Why is the universe so special?' have given us a nudge in the direction of religious belief. The answers we've found do suggest that there's Someone there. I've already agreed that it doesn't amount to proof, but I think there aren't many really important things that can be established in this kind of purely logical and necessary way (just try to *prove* someone's your friend and that they're not being agreeable simply for what they can get out of you, or *prove* that it's wrong to rob a blind man). I'm encouraged to take all this seriously by reflecting that it's not only the rather pious like myself who see things this way. There are a number of scientists, like Paul Davies and Fred Hoyle, who have no sympathy with traditional religious belief, but who, nevertheless, feel that the rational beauty and fruitful balance of the world strongly suggest that there is an intelligence behind

34

it. In fact, Davies goes so far as to say in his book _God and the New Physics_ (Dent, 1992), that 'It may seem bizarre, but in my opinion science offers a surer path to God than religion'. Well, I think this really is bizarre for, although we can learn something of God from the pattern and development of his creation, there are many other things we shall only learn about him if we take the risk and accept the insight of a more personal form of encounter. Meanwhile let's note that, although the scientific detail of this chapter would have surprised (and I'm sure interested) St Paul, its general thrust would not have seemed unfamiliar to him. He once wrote, 'Ever since the creation of the world God's invisible nature, namely, his eternal power and deity, has been clearly perceived in the things that have been made' (Romans 1.20).

3

What's Been Going on?

A couple of years ago, I was sitting in a committee meeting at the Royal Society when someone came in with a telephone message for me. It said, 'Will you appear live on the ITN news at one o'clock today?' It seemed an invitation that would be unlikely to be repeated, so I said 'Yes' and was duly whisked off to the studio. The message did not say why my presence was requested, but I had heard the radio news that morning before setting out for London and I knew what it was all about. The American space agency, NASA, had announced the discovery of 'cosmic ripples'.

They had been using a satellite to look at the background radiation. This is radio noise that fills the universe, and it is a fossil remaining from the state of affairs that existed when the world was about half a million years old. Up until then, the universe had been so hot that radiation interacted so violently with matter that no atoms could survive. When the world had expanded and cooled sufficiently, this was no longer the case. Atoms formed and the radiation was just left lying around, as it were. All that happened to it subsequently was that it continued to cool as the universe continued to expand. It is now very cold (270°C below zero). It provides us with a snapshot of how things were at this very early cosmic age of half a million years, when it first separated from matter.

In fact, everything then was very smooth. Astronomers can find no differences between different parts of the background radiation that are greater than one part in ten thousand. However, it couldn't have been absolutely smooth, otherwise the universe wouldn't have been able eventually to become lumpy with stars and galaxies. There must have been little variations, seeds from which structure was later to grow. The satellite's instruments had discovered just such ripples in this smooth background. An important clue had been obtained as to how the galaxies had come to be.

All this was scientifically very interesting, though scarcely 'the discovery of the century, perhaps of all time' that Stephen Hawking was to call it, most incautiously. However, my job for television was not to explain the science—they had summoned a glamorous lady astronomer to do that—but to answer the question, 'Where does this leave God?' My reply was, 'Exactly where he was before!'

An important theological point lies behind this simple answer. God is not just there to start things off. He's not simply the answer to the question, 'Who lit the blue touch paper of the Big Bang?' This is because creation isn't concerned with how things began, but with what's happening. God is as much the Creator today as he was fifteen billion years ago. He holds the universe in being and his mind and purpose are behind its evolving history. He's the answer to the questions, 'What's been going on?' and 'What does it all mean?'

It's surprising how difficult people seem to find it to grasp this simple point. Back to Stephen Hawking for a moment. He's conjectured a speculative, but highly interesting, theory about the very very early universe, when it was such a tiny fraction of a second old that it was small enough to be influenced by quantum effects. Quantum theory tends to blur things and Hawking's conclusion is that, though the universe has a finite age, its initial quantum fuzziness means it has no dateable beginning. This seems to me to be a plausible conclusion, whatever reservations one might have about the details of Hawking's proposals. Once again, one encounters something that is very interesting scientifically. However, Stephen Hawking thinks that it also has theological consequences. In a famous passage in his book *A Brief History of Time* (Bantam Press 1988), he writes, 'If the universe is really completely self-contained, having no boundary or edge, it would have neither beginning nor end; it would simply be. What place then for a creator?' Actually, it would be theologically naive not to answer, 'Every place, as the Ordainer and Sustainer of all that is going on'. God is not a God of the edges, with a vested interest in beginnings. He is the God of the whole show.

So, if we are to think about God and creation, it is to the 'whole show' that we must turn our attention. In other words, the question of origin in time gives way to the question of what has been happening in cosmic history. It all began very simply. The very early universe is an almost smooth, expanding ball of energy. You can't get much simpler than that. One of the reasons cosmologists can talk with such confidence about the early universe is because it is, in fact, a very uncomplicated system. However, this world, which started so simple, has, after fifteen billion years, become immensely rich and complicated. You and I are the most complicated known consequences of this fruitful history. A universe that, when it was a ten thousand millionth of a second old, was just a hot soup of elementary particles, has become the home of saints and scientists. Remember, this has only been possible because the universe has anthropic fine tuning built into its physical fabric. Such astonishing fertility doesn't look like a purposeless world of accident.

Yet, wait a minute! A closer inspection of the history of the universe reveals a more puzzling and problematic picture. We understand a good many of the processes by which this rich complexity has been evolved. Each one of them seems characterized by an interplay between two opposing tendencies that, in a slogan kind of a way, one could call 'chance and necessity'. These are slippery words, so I'd better define what I mean by them. By 'chance' I mean happenstance, the way things happen to be, that they are this way rather than that way. By 'necessity' I mean the lawful regularity that governs how things develop. A couple of examples will make things clearer.

As we've seen, the early universe wasn't completely smooth, there were ripples in which there was a bit more matter here than elsewhere. These fluctuations are chance, happenstance. They are augmented by necessity, the lawful force of gravity. A bit more matter exerts a bit more gravitational pull, which attracts a bit more matter in its turn. A snowballing process has begun by which the universe, after about a billion years, became lumpy with galaxies and the galaxies became lumpy with stars.

More familiar is the story of biological evolution. Genetic mutations are happenstance, they just occur from time to time. Thus, there arise new forms of life that are sifted and preserved by natural selection in an orderly environment. If genetic information were unchangingly transmitted from generation to generation, nothing new would ever happen, and, if it were not reasonably reliable in its transmission, nothing would ever be perpetuated. A fertile world must be neither too rigid, nor too loose. It needs both chance and necessity.

Chance is the engine of novelty. Necessity is the preserver of fruitfulness. This much is plain. However, doesn't the role of chance deny the theological claim that universal history is the unfolding of a divine purpose? Biologists, particularly, have tended to see it this way. Apparently, they are less impressed by (even, possibly, less aware of?) the finely tuned groundrules of the cosmic game than are their physical colleagues. The Nobel Prize-winning French biochemist Jacques Monod, in a book called *Chance and Necessity* (Collins, 1972), looked at evolutionary history and concluded that, 'man at last knows he is alone in the unfeeling immensity of the universe, out of which he has emerged by chance'. For Monod, the universe's history is a tale told by an idiot. It is chance that makes it so.

Do we have to read it this way, though? I think not. What science tells us about the world and its history constrains what we may go on to believe about questions of deeper meaning and purpose, but it does not, by itself, determine what the answers to these questions should be. There is room for metaphysical manoeuvre, and whether or not we reach theistic or atheistic conclusions will depend upon wider considerations. In the previous chapter, I sought to show how the rational beauty and fine tuning of the universe could be seen as supportive of belief in God, without claiming that such belief was *demanded* by any kind of proof positive. In a similar way, I do not believe that Monod, and those who follow him, like Richard Dawkins in *The Blind Watchmaker* (Longman, 1986), can claim that they have *proved* their atheistic case. In the end, we have to assess what makes the best sense overall. Let me offer an alternative interpretation of the role of chance and necessity.

I would like to suggest, respectfully, that when God came to create the world, he faced a dilemma. God is faithful, and the natural gift of the faithful God will be reliability in the operation of his creation. However, reliability by itself could harden into mere rigidity, leading to a clockwork world in which nothing really new ever happened. God is also loving, and the natural gift of the loving God will be an independence granted to his creation. We know this as parents. There comes a time when every child has to be allowed to go off on their bicycle, on their own, into the precarious world of traffic. Parental letting-be is an indispensable gift to

give in the process of growing-up. Independence
on its own, however, could degenerate into mere
licence, leading to a world of disorderly chaos.

I believe that the God who is both loving and
faithful has given to his creation the twin gifts of
independence *and* reliability. These find their reflection in the fruitful interplay of chance and necessity
in evolving cosmic history. Such an account gives
a much more positive understanding of the role of
chance. Monod and Dawkins like to apply to chance
the adjective 'blind', suggestive of purposelessness
and meaninglessness, but we do not need to be
beguiled by their tendentious choice of words. The
shuffling operations of happenstance are a way of
exploring and bringing to light the deep anthropic
fruitfulness with which the physical world has been
endowed. Arthur Peacocke, who is a biochemist and
Anglican priest, writes in *Creation and the World of
Science* (OUP, 1979) of chance as, 'the search radar
of God, sweeping through all possible targets of its
probing'.

There are two extreme pictures of God's relationship to creation that are unacceptable to Christian
theology. One is the picture of the universe as God's
puppet theatre, in which he pulls every string and
makes all creatures dance to his tune alone. The God
of love cannot be such a cosmic tyrant, but neither
can he be an indifferent spectator, who just set it all
going, then left the universe to get on with it. We
have to strive for an understanding that lies in
between these two extremes. Cosmic history is not
the unfolding of an inexorable divine plan. An evolutionary world is to be understood theologically as

a world allowed by the Creator to make itself to a large degree. Yet, this self-making takes place in a setting of finely tuned potentiality, and I believe that God providentially interacts with its history (this last point is one I shall take up in a later chapter). In other words, creation is not the starting off of something that is produced ready-made; rather, it is a *continuous process.* As I said earlier, God is as much the Creator today as he was fifteen billion years ago.

Because continuous creation allows room for creaturely freedom within this process, the consequences will be lots of things that have come about 'by chance' in the course of history. I do not believe that it was laid down from the foundation of the world that humankind should have five fingers—it has just worked out that way—but I by no means believe that it is pure accident that beings capable of self-consciousness and of worship have emerged in the course of cosmic history. In other words, there is a general overall purpose being fulfilled in what is going on, but the details of what actually occurs are left to the contingencies of history (this happening rather than that). The picture is of a world endowed with fruitfulness, guided by its Creator, but allowed an ability to realize this fruitfulness in its own particular ways. Chance is a sign of freedom, not blind purposelessness.

A universe of this character is bound to be a world with ragged edges. The shuffling explorations of chance will lead to deterioration as well as fruitful novelty, to blind alleys as well as ways ahead. Here we begin to make contact with the great question mark that hangs over all that has been going on in the history of the world. I refer, of course, to the problem of evil and suffering. It scarcely needs elaborating, for none of us live free from its perplexing nature. We all know people whose lives have been diminished or cut short by unmerited ill-fortune. Does a world with cancer and concentration camps really look like the creation of a powerful and loving God? I think this is the difficulty that, more than any other, holds people back from belief in God. Those of us who hold this belief are, nevertheless, always aware of the deep problems that the bitterness of human experience poses for us.

There are really two problems. One is what is usually called moral evil, the chosen cruelties and neglects of humankind. How, though, can one have a world in which humans are free to choose without some of these choices being for ill rather than for good? We are moral beings, with all the possibilities for immorality that this implies, not perfectly programmed automata. No doubt our choices are often subject to pressures from our society, which pushes us in evil directions. As I write, a grievous civil war is going on in Bosnia. In this conflict, individuals on all sides are committing acts of atrocity, partly from personal hatred, partly from involvement in their community, with its accumulated memories of unsettled scores arising from evils inflicted on it in the past. Individually and collectively, human choices are the source of much suffering. However, our moral instincts are that human beings are not to be turned into automata. We recoil from coercive methods (such as the enforced castration of persistent sex offenders) that would have such an end in view. Philosophers call this insight 'the free will defence', meaning that the possibility of moral evil is the price that must be paid for the greater good of human freedom.

Even if you can agree with this, there remains the second problem. It concerns physical evil, the diseases and disasters that are our common lot. Some of the effects of this kind of evil may be exacerbated by human wrongdoing—such as when we heedlessly pollute the environment with carcinogens, or build schools on earthquake faults because the land is cheap—but the principal responsibility here is not ours. To put it bluntly, surely the responsibility for physical evil rests with God. He created the world as it is. What can be said in his defence?

We tend to believe that if we had been in charge of creation we would have done it better. With a little more care about the details, we would have kept the beauty of sunsets, but eliminated germs like staphylococci. The more we understand the processes of the world, however, the less likely does it seem that this would be possible. The created order looks like a package deal. Exactly the same biochemical processes that enable cells to mutate, making evolution possible, are those that enable cells to become cancerous and generate tumours. You can't have one without the other. In other words, the possibility of disease is not gratuitous, it's the necessary cost of life.

This is so if the universe is to be orderly. Of course, God might have created a magic world in which he intervened every time a cell looked like becoming malignant, or our hands got too near the dangerous fire. No doubt it was not beyond God's power to do this, but I think it would have been contrary to his character. It is important to understand what we mean when we call God 'almighty'. We don't just mean he can do anything he pleases, as if we understood this in some sort of whimsical way. What actually pleases him is in accord with the kind of being he is. The rational God will create a rational universe. He did not create a magic world because he is not a magician. Such a world could not have been the home of morally responsible beings, because in such a world there would be no true consequences of our deeds. I would not need to bother about diligently servicing the aeroplane in which you are about to travel, or about taking care of you when you are ill. If I made a mess of these responsibilities, so what? God would put it all right, whatever happened.

A world in which God perpetually intervened in this magical way would also not be a creation that he would be allowing freely to be itself. An Oxford theologian, Austin Farrer, once asked himself what was God's will in the Lisbon earthquake? This terrible disaster took place on All Saints Day in 1755. The churches were full and they all collapsed, killing 50 thousand people. It was a most bitter example of natural evil. Farrer's answer was hard, but true. God's will was that the elements of the Earth's crust should behave in accordance with their nature. In other words, they are allowed to be in their own way, just as we are allowed to be in ours.

I have called this insight 'the free process defence'.

It bears the same relation to natural evil that the free will defence does to moral evil. 'But wait a minute', I hear you say, 'there may be some moral worth in allowing human beings freedom, but what's the point in doing the same for tectonic plates? In fact, isn't it just an abuse of language to apply a word like 'free' to such inanimate objects?' I see what you're getting at, but, once again, I suspect that things can't be separated from each other in quite so neat a way. You see, we're characters in the cosmic play who have emerged from the scenery. Animate beings have evolved from inanimate matter, and our nature is tied to that of the physical world, which gave us birth. Once again, I suspect it is a package deal. Only a universe to which the free process defence applied could be expected to give rise to beings to whom the free will defence applies.

I do not believe that God directly wills either the act of a murderer, or the incidence of a cancer. I believe he allows both to happen in a creation to which he has given the gift of being itself.

If these ideas are right, they show us that the suffering and evil of the world are not due to weakness, oversight, or callousness on God's part, but, rather, they are the inescapable cost of a creation allowed to be other than God, released from tight divine control, and permitted to be itself. However, the mystery of suffering remains. When mortal illness strikes a young mother, it is certainly not to be seen as some horrible form of divine punishment, or a consequence of divine indifference, but the tragedy of this situation is not removed simply by noting that the possibility of cancer is the necessary price of the evolution of new life. A profound problem remains, beyond the reach of intellectual argument alone.

One of my main reasons for being a Christian is that Christianity speaks to the problem of suffering at the deepest possible level. The Christian God is not just a compassionate spectator, looking down in pity on the bitterness of the strange world that he has made. We believe that he has been a fellow participant in the world's suffering, that he knows it from the inside and does not just sympathize with it from the outside. This is one of the meanings of the cross of Christ.

Christians believe that God has shared our lot by living a truly human life in Jesus Christ. This is a tremendous and exciting claim. It means that God has acted to make himself known to us in the plainest possible terms, namely through a human life and a human death. It is also a profoundly mysterious claim. I have tried elsewhere (for example, in *The Way the World Is*) to explain why I think this is true. I won't repeat the discussion here, but, for the present, just note that, from the earliest documents of the New Testament onwards, Christians have never been able to express their experience of Jesus Christ without feeling the need to use divine language as well as human language, however difficult this combination may be to understand. It's a bit like the physicists with light, mentioned earlier—they knew they had to use both wave language and particle language about it long before they knew how the two could be reconciled. Sometimes one just has to hold on by the skin of one's intellectual teeth to the strange way things turn out to be.

If this understanding of Jesus is true, then in that lonely figure hanging on the cross, we see God himself accepting suffering, and opening his arms to embrace the bitterness of the world. He is not above us in our misery, but alongside us in its darkness. Once, in the concentration camps of World War II, a young Jewish boy hung, twisting and dying in a Gestapo noose. From the crowd of his fellow Jews, forced to witness the execution, came the cry 'Where is God now?' One of them tells us that he felt inside him the answer, 'He is here, hanging in the noose'. This insight, of God as the fellow sufferer, that Christians believe was historically acted out in the cross of Jesus Christ, meets the problem of suffering at the profoundest possible level.

There is another thing to say. We have been thinking about evil and suffering. We should also think about hope. Despite the darkness of so much human experience, there is also within us a deep intuition that, in the end, all will be well. When in the night a mother comforts a frightened child with the words, 'It's all right,' we do not believe that she is uttering a loving lie. Rather, we know that this reassurance is fundamental to the human growth and development of the child. I believe this is because it represents a true insight into the way things are. Despite all appearances to the contrary, reality is on our side. We are not 'alone in an unfeeling universe'; the world is our home. I don't see how this can be unless, behind the fruitfulness and futilities of cosmic history, there is the benevolent will and purpose of the God of steadfast love.

In conclusion, perhaps I had better say something

49

about where the first two chapters of Genesis fit into what I've been saying. The Bible is very important to me and I give it great respect. Part of this respect is to try to figure out exactly what it is I'm reading. You see, the Bible is not a book, it's a library. In this library we can find all sorts of writings: poetry and prose, history and story, laws, letters and so on. It's a great mistake to read poetry as if it were prose. When Robert Burns says that his love is like a red, red rose, he doesn't mean he's in love with Ena Harkness, or that his girlfriend has green leaves and prickles.

It's a great mistake to read Genesis 1 and 2 as if they were a divinely guaranteed scientific textbook. In fact, they're something more interesting than this. They're *theological* writing, and their main purpose is to assert that all that exists does so because of the will of God (God said 'let there be . . . '). The early Christians knew this and it was only in later medieval and Reformation times that people began to insist on a literal interpretation. When science made this no longer possible, Genesis 1 and 2 were liberated to play their proper theological role again. In fact, God didn't produce a ready-made world. He's done something cleverer than this. He's created a world able to make itself.

4

Who Are We?

When I started research in theoretical physics, many years ago, we believed that matter consisted of atoms made up of electrons going round a nucleus, and that the nucleus itself was made up of particles called protons and neutrons. In the course of my twenty-five years or so working in the area, we learned that protons and neutrons are themselves made up of yet smaller particles. These are the celebrated quarks and the particles that make them stick together, which are called (oh dear!) gluons. This is typically how physics proceeds. It pulls things apart into smaller and smaller pieces. We have learned all sorts of worthwhile and interesting things this way. The question is whether or not it is the only way to learn what things are *really* like. In the end, are we just immensely complicated collections of quarks, gluons, and electrons?

People who answer 'Yes' to this last question are called reductionists. In their view, the whole reduces simply to a collection of the parts. They are sometimes also called 'nothing butters', for they believe we are 'nothing but' collections of elementary particles. Those of us who do not share this view are called antireductionists. We believe that 'more is different', that the whole is more than simply the sum of its parts. If you are a reductionist, physics is *the* fundamental subject and the rest—biology, anthropology, and so on—are (very complicated) consequences of it. If you are an antireductionist you take a much broader view of reality and believe, for instance, that biology will never become simply complicated physics.

This doesn't mean that you think that bringing about life requires the addition of some sort of extra magic ingredient to ordinary matter. This kind of view is called 'vitalism', and the more we understand the biochemistry of life, the more unlikely it seems that it is true. One important reason for saying this is that there seems to be a continuous story from the chemically rich shallow pools of early Earth, to the first elementary replicating and living systems, and then on through biological evolution to you and me. We certainly don't understand all the stages of this fruitful history. In particular, the biochemical pathways by which life got going are not currently known, but it seems a good bet that it was a continuous process, which, one day, we may hope to understand.

If this is correct, the novelty that makes 'more different' arises, not from the injection of something extra from the *outside*, but from the effects of greater complexity on the *inside*. In other words, entirely new properties emerge as systems become more and more complicated, properties that could have no meaning in terms of the simple parts by themselves. A very easy example of this is the wetness of water. A few H_2O molecules by themselves are not wet, but, if you have a collection of billions of these molecules, they interact with each other in such a way as to produce an energy at the surface of the collection that physicists call surface tension and we experience as wetness.

It's rather easy to see in outline (even if difficult to figure out in detail) how such a property as wetness could emerge. It is a collective effect of all the water molecules together. Wetness is an energetic property, and, as all the molecules have some energy, the way they share it can be expected to change when they're brought together. Energy is distributed between them in a new way. There's nothing very profound in the emergence of wetness.

Much more profound is the emergence of a property like consciousness. In fact, this is the most surprising and significant thing that's happened in the whole history of the universe. A world that was once just an expanding ball of energy has become aware of itself, so that, through us, the universe *knows* that it was once an expanding ball of energy. Consciousness is surely more than an effect of patterns of energy. Here's something infinitely more mysterious than mere wetness.

I don't think that this mystery begins to be removed by the remarkable advances of either neurophysiology (the study of biochemical processes of the brain) or artificial intelligence (the achievements of computers in processing vast quantities of information). Impressive as these developments have been, they do not even begin to chip away at the mystery of consciousness. There's a yawning gap between talk of neural networks in the brain (however sophisticated such talk may be), and the most elementary mental experience of perceiving, say, a patch of pink. The essence of consciousness is awareness. Only if we thought a computer was aware would we think it unethical to pull its plug out of the power supply.

We shouldn't be misled by the triumphalist and unsubstantiated claims of the reductionists that the age-old problem of mind and brain is about to be solved. Of course, there's an intimate connection between the two. A smart tap on the head with a hammer will establish the point quickly enough by the effect this act will have on my thinking processes. Yet thought is different to the firing of complicated patterns of neurons; the mind is not just 'what the brain does' in simplistic physical terms. The emergence of consciousness is something more radically novel than can be explained in terms of energy alone. I believe we're centuries away from an understanding of what's actually going on, all the time, in our conscious experience. It's linked with what's going on in our skulls, but is not simply identical to neural activity.

I don't rejoice in our current ignorance in these matters, but honesty requires us to acknowledge it. Yet, even in our intellectual darkness, there are one or two tiny glimmers of light. They arise from the perception by twentieth-century science that the physical world is, first, not mechanical and, second, interconnected. These two properties have shown up both at the subatomic level, where processes are inherently quantum mechanical, and also at the everyday level, where processes are much as Newton described them, but more interesting than he realized.

Quantum mechanics is notorious for its fitfulness. We cannot tell precisely what the outcome of a quantum event will be. If we look for an electron, we may find it 'here' or we may find it 'there'. We can assign probabilities for these discoveries—so that, maybe, we can predict that most of the time when we look, it will be found 'here'—but we cannot say where it will actually be located on any particular occasion on which we try to find this out. Such radical randomness makes the quantum world unpredictable and unmechanical. Yet, when we add together the behaviours of lots of quantum particles (as we have to do for even a tiny piece of matter), these variations and uncertainties tend to cancel each other out, producing a highly reliable pattern of overall behaviour. It is rather like life assurance. The actuaries don't know when you're going to die; they only know the probability of death for someone of your age in the course of the next few years. Provided they collect premiums from enough people, this is sufficient for the insurance offices to be able to make money. Whatever the individual fluctuations, the behaviour of a big enough group will still be sufficiently predictable.

More interesting for our present purpose is another, less well-known, property of quantum theory. Once two electrons (or any other pair of quantum particles) have interacted with each other, they possess a power to influence each other, however widely they subsequently separate. If one electron stays around here in the laboratory and the other goes 'beyond the Moon' (as we say), then anything I do to the electron here will have an immediate effect on its distant brother. In other words, there's a very surprising 'togetherness in separation' built into the fabric of the quantum world. Einstein was one of the first people to see that this was so, and he thought it was so crazy that he believed that it showed there must be something wrong with quantum theory (although Einstein had been a kind of grandfather of quantum mechanics, he didn't like its later developments, and he was always trying to discredit it). However, about ten years ago, some Frenchmen did some very clever experiments that showed that this strange togetherness is indeed the case (of course, they didn't send an electron beyond the Moon, but they figured out how to test the idea in a less dramatic way). In the trade, we call this effect the 'EPR experiment', because Einstein did the original work with two young collaborators, Boris Podolsky and Nathan Rosen. For more details see chapter 7 of my *The Quantum World*.

Something very significant is happening here. Elementary particle physicists try to tear things apart, but physical reality, it seems, fights back. The EPR experiment shows that the subatomic world cannot be treated atomistically. There's an intrinsic interconnectedness that cannot be broken. People are still trying to work out all the implications of this astonishing discovery.

In a different way, we find similar characteristics in the everyday, large-scale world of our direct physical experience. Its behaviour is described by laws that Newton discovered over 300 years ago. We thought we understood these laws pretty well, but, in this century, we have found that they have consequences no one had anticipated. Like most physicists, I learned about classical mechanics (as we call this branch of physics) by studying simple systems, like a steadily oscillating pendulum. Something like this is pretty robust, by which I mean that if you slightly disturb the pendulum, it will only slightly affect the way it oscillates. A system like this is tame, that is, controllable and predictable. In a word it is mechanical. We once thought that all the everyday world was like this. We now know that we were wrong. Our everyday world does have some clocks in it, but almost all of it is clouds. By this I mean that most systems are so exquisitely sensitive to circumstance that the slightest disturbance will make them behave in some totally different way. This surprising discovery is sometimes called 'the butterfly effect'. You won't be astonished to learn that one of the earliest examples of this behaviour came to light during attempts to understand the Earth's weather systems. They are so sensitive that a butterfly stirring the air with its wings in the African jungle today will have consequences for the storms over London in three or four weeks' time. Because we can't know about all these African butterflies, I can say with confidence that detailed long-term weather forecasting is never going to work!

I'll talk some more in the next chapter about what significance we should attribute to these discoveries, but for the moment, let us be content to note two immediate consequences. These exquisitely sensitive systems are intrinsically unpredictable and nonmechanical in their behaviour. They're also never truly separable from their environment, for they are vulnerable to changes that result from the slightest of variations in their circumstances. Once again, the reductionist programme of splitting the world up into lots of little separate pieces is found not to work.

These insights are mere glimmers in the gloom of ignorance about what we really are, but they certainly do not encourage some crude form of the 'nothing buttery' kind of thinking. Reality is built up from relationships. Wholes have a significance exceeding that of the bits that make them up. Yet, the world is full of scientists who go round making grossly improbable claims, such as human beings are 'genetic survival machines', or 'computers made of meat'. The insights gained via their particular disciplines, which have their rightful *parts* in our attempts at knowledge of the whole, are blown up into some crass and improbable rules for everything. It is mostly biologists and cognitive scientists who make such claims. Why do they do it?

Well, we've been here before, but last time round it was the physicists, in the second half of the eighteenth century, who were the 'nothing butters'. The great discoveries of Newton had been followed up and exploited. It seemed to his followers, as it had never seemed to Newton himself, that the physical world (by which was largely meant the solar system of the Sun and its encircling planets) was a gigantic piece of clockwork. So, *everything* must be clockwork . . . People wrote books with titles like *Man the Machine*. We've already seen what a mistake this was, for the Newtonian world has many more clouds than clocks in it. However, even though this is the case, it's the clocks that one understands first because they're so much easier than those exquisitely sensitive clouds. Then, the temptation is to make these early, mechanical discoveries into a pattern for *all* knowledge.

I think much the same thing has been happening with biology in the second half of the twentieth century. It has scored its first great, stunning, quantitative success in unravelling the molecular basis of genetics. Rightly, the biologists feel pretty pleased with themselves. Yet, a degree of sobriety and caution is also called for. The structure of DNA, and the transmission of genetic information is essentially a mechanical problem (this is why Crick and Watson could make their famous model of the double helix out of bits of metal). It doesn't follow from this that *all* aspects of life are mechanical, or that biology is just large-scale physics, pure and simple.

We don't understand what we are, but we should resist any impoverished account of human nature that denies or trivializes basic human experience. Of course, we're part of the physical world, and so the scientists, with their emphasis on the repeatable and the measurable, will have things to tell us about what we are, but we must also pay attention to the artists, for the fact that the world is the carrier of beauty is surely deeply significant. I don't think that our aesthetic experience is just an emotional by-product of the 'hard wiring' of our brains. It is not just a peculiar human phenomenon of merely accidental origin. Rather, art is a window into reality, providing its own vital perspective on the way things are.

We must also pay attention to the writers. At their most profound, they portray for us a world that is the arena of moral choice and responsibility. I certainly understand that there are cultural elements in ethical systems, but I can't believe that my conviction that torturing children is wrong is just a conventional agreement of my society to see things this way. I believe I know, as surely as I know anything, that love is better than hate, truth is better than the lie.

We must also pay attention to the saints and mystics. Modern Western unbelief is an historical and geographical oddity. Throughout the world, and throughout history, there is impressive human testimony to encounters with a Reality, both beyond us and yet also nearer to us than breathing, of one who meets humanity with judgement and mercy.

Reductionists will try to explain away these nonscientific aspects of human experience. There is no place for them in the cold, hard, lifeless world of the reductionist account. For this account, music really *is* just vibrations in the air; the *Mona Lisa* really *is* just a collection of specks of paint of known chemical composition. Ethical intentions and religious intimations are just strategies for survival, programmed into us by the selfish genes. It is hard to exaggerate the implausibility of this limited view of reality. All that is most profound, all that makes human life worth living, is devalued and discarded, sacrificed to an unjustified scientific imperialism. The personal is treated as mere froth on the surface

of matter. Even the experience of wonder, so fundamental in the scientific life, will find no home in this
bleak story.

The world in which we actually live is multilayered in the richness of its reality. One of the
attractions of a religious account is that, in seeing
the will and nature of the Creator underlying and
unifying the varieties of human experience, it makes
this richness more intelligible. Our scientific explorations are insights into the rational order with
which God has endowed his universe. Our experiences of beauty are a sharing in his joy in creation.
Our moral perceptions are intuitions of his good
and perfect will. Our religious experiences are
encounters with his hidden presence. Such a view
is whole and satisfying. It has the ring of truth about
it. Who are we? We are God's creatures.

5

Can a Scientist Pray?

I suppose it depends a bit on what you mean by prayer. Scientists habitually experience wonder at the beauty of the physical world, and this is a kind of prayer, whether you know it or not. Yet, when one asks the question which is the title of this chapter, it's petitionary prayer—asking God for something—that first springs to the minds of most of us. In the New Testament, we're encouraged to 'make our requests known to God'. Jesus says things like 'Ask and it will be given you'. Prayer is a very natural human activity. There can be few who have never uttered a petition.

I became more acutely aware than ever of the need to pray when I started hospital visiting. The patients I went to see were all acutely ill, and some of them seemed close to death. It was impossible *not* to pray for them. I did not do so expecting that each would be granted some instant miracle, but, rather, as a way of sharing in their experience, and of seeking God's grace and presence for them in what was happening, which might bring either recovery, or the acceptance of death.

I learned that this form of prayer is truly effective when I was seriously ill myself. My life was greatly diminished, reduced to my hospital bed, and the drips that were keeping me alive. God felt almost infinitely distant, but I was very conscious of, and sustained by, the prayers of those I knew would be remembering me. When I could not pray much myself, they did something real for me.

Ultimately, though, was all this just a bit of comforting psychology? Can we really pray today in a way that asks things of God? In a drought, could we pray for a change in the weather? When people believed that rain came from turning on the heavenly tap, it might have made sense to do so. Now we're a bit more sophisticated. Doesn't the weather just *happen*? Hasn't science shown us that the world is so orderly and regular that there's no room left for God to do anything in particular?

Three things—one scientific, one human, one religious—should make us pause before dismissing this matter quite so quickly. The scientific one first.

If the world were mechanized, a kind of gigantic piece of clockwork, with God being the great unseen clockmaker, then, no doubt, it would all just tick away and we'd have to hope that he'd wound it up so cleverly that things wouldn't turn out too badly. The last chapter, though, showed us that modern science doesn't describe the world like this at all. It is much more subtle and, maybe, also more supple than this. The weather is incredibly complicated, in a way that makes it impossible to say exactly what will or will not make it rain next Saturday. Remember all those African butterflies. The smallest triggers can have the largest eventual effects.

Next, we didn't actually need modern science to tell us that it's not all mechanical, for we've always known—as surely as we know anything—that *we* are not automata. I know some philosophers deny this, but the experience of real choice—and, hence, of real responsibility—is basic to being human. Yet, we're also part of the physical world. This means that the processes of the world cannot be so tightly knit that there is no room for our manoeuvre within them. If *we* can act in a world that is sufficiently open to the future for this to be possible, may it not also be the case that *God* can act in it also?

The final point is religious. Christianity, and Judaism and Islam, speak of God in personal terms. Now, we know that when we finite human beings talk about the infinite God, our language and understanding are not really adequate to the task. Our words have to be stretched in some way, even to begin to meet the case. Nevertheless, it is personal language that seems the least inadequate for this purpose. God is thought of as 'Father', not as 'Force'. This doesn't mean, of course, that he's an old gentleman with a long white beard, up above the bright blue sky. No one thinks that. However, it seems to me that it does mean that God is one who cares, who takes a personal and individual interest in his creatures. How can God be Father in this way unless he is able to do particular things on particular occasions, in particular circumstances? He is not just the God of the whole big show, he is also the God of Abraham, Isaac, and Jacob, of you, and me. Such a God must be able to do specific things. The laws of nature (which, after all, are themselves just general expressions of the will of the faithful Creator) cannot be such as to prevent him from interacting with his creation.

Thus, we have strong motivation for trying to see how it is that we and God are both able to act in the world. I have to admit limited understanding; we don't know how our mental acts of willing our arms to raise result in the physical actions of their being raised. We don't know how mind and brain relate. We're ignorant, and so we have to make guesses. I think we'll see two things in the course of doing so. One is that we *can* make some sort of conjecture about how actions happen; the other is that the kind of guess that might work for human acts will be a useful clue as to how to think about divine acts as well. The key to it all, I believe, lies in the exquisite sensitivity that so much of the everyday physical world possesses. In other words, we're not clocks because there are so many clouds around.

This sensitivity is such an important point that the time has come to give an example of it. Let's take the air around us. As you know, it consists of lots of little molecules, all whizzing about and colliding with each other. In fact, in one ten thousand millionth of a second (a pretty short time), each molecule has had about fifty collisions with its neighbours. Now, the molecules aren't exactly little round billiard balls, but the way they collide is just the same as if they were. Consequently, we can use a billiard ball model to describe the situation. We now pose the following question. How accurately do we have to know things at the beginning in order to be able to predict how one of these molecules will be moving one ten thousand millionth of a second later, after its fifty collisions? The impact of two billiard balls is a problem that Newton himself solved. He gave us a perfectly definite answer, *provided we know exactly how the two balls collided.* However, a little uncertainty about their initial directions will produce a much greater uncertainty about the directions in which they separate (anyone who has played snooker knows that a small error in cueing produces a disastrous error in the shot). This is the case for *one* collision. For many successive collisions, these errors multiply at an alarming rate (technically speaking, they exponentiate). A simple calculation leads to the following astonishing conclusion: for air molecules, in so short a time as one ten thousand millionth of a second, we shall make a serious error in our calculation if we have failed to take into account the effect of an electron (the smallest particle of matter) on the other side of the observable universe (about as far away as you can get) interacting with the air by means of gravitational attraction (the weakest of the forces of nature). In other words, even for a simple system like air, for a period that is a very tiny fraction of a second, its detailed behaviour is absolutely unpredictable without literally universal knowledge. *This* is what one means by exquisite sensitivity. These systems are unpredictable in behaviour because they can never be insulated from the smallest nudges given them by their environment.

The scientific account of systems of this kind has been given the name of chaos theory. It was rather an unfortunate choice of title, for, while their behaviour exhibits a degree of apparent randomness, these systems also exhibit a degree of order. We cannot say what such a system will do next, but its range of immediate possibilities is contained within certain bounds. In the jargon of the subject, we say that its motion will not take it absolutely anywhere, but it is confined to a 'strange attractor'. I won't attempt to go into details, but notice that chaos theory is an odd mixture of order and disorder, of randomness contained within a patterned structure.

What are we to make of all this? Remember that we started out with Newton's laws, which are mechanical and deterministic in character—that, when two billiard balls collided, if we knew exactly how they did so, we could calculate exactly how they separated. Unpredictability and apparent randomness resulted from the extreme sensitivity to the (essentially unknowable) fine details of what was going on. So, is it all just a question of ignorance? The weather really *is* determined and it's only our lack of knowledge of the flappings of African butterflies that prevents our working out what it will be next month. Or is it something more interesting than that?

At this point, we face a choice as to what sort of guess to make. We can suppose that Newton was exactly right, and so all our problems are those of ignorance, or we can suppose that this radical unpredictability is a sign that nature is more subtle and supple than we had hitherto recognized. My instincts as a scientist encourage me to make the latter guess.

Scientists are realists; they believe that what we know, or what we can't know, show us what things are really like. My wife gave me a sweatshirt recently with the stirring motto 'Epistemology

Models Ontology', or, in less learned language, what we can know is a reliable guide to what is the case. You can see how natural this is for a scientist by recalling an early episode in the history of quantum theory. It concerns Heisenberg's celebrated Uncertainty Principle, which we met earlier, that tells us that if we know where an electron is, we can't know what it's doing, and if we know what it's doing, we can't know where it is. When Heisenberg made this great discovery, he did so by figuring out what you could actually *measure*. If you measured position absolutely accurately, you disturbed things so that you made the momentum completely uncertain, and vice versa. In other words, he was concerned with what one could *know*, with epistemology as philosophers say. However, very soon afterwards, Heisenberg and nearly all other physicists were interpreting the Uncertainty Principle, not as a principle of ignorance, but as a principle of indeterminacy. It wasn't just that you couldn't know the electron's momentum if you had fixed its position, it was that it just didn't have a definite momentum to be known. In other words, it was a question of what was (or was not) the case. The physicists had moved from epistemology to ontology.

I suggest we do the same with chaos theory. The way this might work out would be something like this. The sensitivity of chaotic systems means that they can never be isolated from what goes on around them. This implies that they can only properly be discussed holistically, that is to say in terms of *all* that is going on, not just in terms of localized bits and pieces. The way they react to small nudges corresponds not to a change in energy (for the nudges can be vanishingly small), but to a change in the pattern of behaviour within the confines of possibility represented by the 'strange attractor'. Of course, it is also possible to change their behaviour by inputs of energy, as when the weather is affected by a volcanic eruption rather than the flapping of a butterfly's wings, but it's the non-energetic changes that are more significant for us in this chapter.

From this we derive a picture of two sorts of causality acting in the physical world. One is the kind with which scientists have long been familiar—inputs of energy, described by conventional physics in terms of the behaviour of the parts. Because this involves localized interactions with constituent bits, we could call it 'bottom-up causality'. The other is a new kind, at least as far as physics is concerned—inputs of pattern formation ('information' is the technical word used for it), described in terms of the overall behaviour of the whole. We could call this 'top-down causality'. On this understanding, the future of these sensitive, intrinsically unpredictable, chaotic systems is open, not in the sense that it results in some sort of whimsically random outcome, but in the sense that additional causal principles are free to operate, of the top-down kind, *and* the familiar bottom-up causal principles described by a reductionist science. We have reason to believe that the latter do not draw the grain of nature so tight as to exclude a role for the former kind of causality.

Before I go on to discuss some of the consequences of this picture of the world, I must deal with a point that is probably troubling you. I have described this picture as a 'guess', and I have talked solely about the Newtonian physics of the everyday world. Yet, these exquisitely sensitive systems soon depend upon fine details of their circumstance, of a kind that Heisenberg's Uncertainty Principle declares to be indeterminate. Will not this enmeshment with quantum uncertainty already settle the question for us? Does it not tell us that the future is inescapably open? Maybe. The reasons for my hesitation in simply calling in quantum theory to settle the matter are of a rather technical kind. Essentially, we do not understand how the quantum world and the everyday world interlock with each other. For those in the know, the perplexities relate to the unsolved problem of how measurements are made (see Chapter 6 of my *The Quantum World* (Penguin, 1990) for a typical discussion of the issues). Until we get this settled, we must be a little wary of using quantum scissors to cut the Gordian knot of everyday causality.

After that cautious excursion, let us return to thinking about top-down causality. It might take at least three forms.

First, there may be holistic laws of nature that explain the very remarkable drive towards complexity exhibited in the course of cosmic and terrestrial history. Many physical scientists suspect that the neo-Darwinian account of the natural selection of genetic mutations is only part of the story of the amazingly rapid development of life. If there are such top-down laws, it is certainly science's job to seek to identify them.

Second, notions of top-down causality within the ultra-complex area of the brain, begin to offer a glimmer of understanding of how it might be that we are able to execute our mental intentions through the physical actions of our bodies. I do not for one moment claim that the mystery of mind and brain is near to a solution, but one major attraction of the 'guess' I have been suggesting is that it begins to describe a physical world that we can conceive ourselves as inhabiting. The way we act in our bodies seems to have this holistic, top-down, character to it.

Third, there is much cloudy unpredictable process throughout the whole of the physical world. It is a coherent possibility that God interacts with the history of his creation by means of 'information input' into its open physical process. The causal net of the universe is not drawn so tight as to exclude this possibility. Mere mechanism is dead and a more subtle and supple universe is accessible to the providential interaction of the Creator.

There are those who say, 'Is this not a return to a God of the gaps?' To answer this, one has to ask, 'What was wrong with that idea?' The trouble was that the gaps being appealed to then were just patches of contemporary ignorance. With the advance of knowledge they, and the God associated with them, just faded away. However, if there is a real openness, permitting both top-down and bottom-up causality, there will have to be *intrinsic* gaps in the bottom-up description alone in order to leave room for top-down action. There can be no objection to gaps of this kind. We are people of the gaps, and God can be a God of these gaps, in a perfectly acceptable way.

If this picture of divine agency is right, a number of consequences flow from it.

First, divine action will always be hidden, for it will be contained within the cloudiness of unpredictable processes. The sensitivity of these processes implies that the different forms of causality present can never be separately identified and disentangled from one another. One cannot say, 'This event was due to nature', and, 'That event was due to divine providence'. This seems to me to be the appropriate reflection in the physical world of that theological necessity we discussed earlier, that God neither does everything nor does he do nothing, but he interacts, patiently and lovingly, with the process of his creation, to which he had given its own due measure of independence. This intermingling of providential grace with the freedom of nature means that divine action will not be demonstrable by experiment, though it may be discernible by the intuition of faith.

Second, though there are many clouds in the world, there are also some clocks. The regularity of the mechanical aspects of nature are to be understood theologically as signs of the faithfulness of the Creator. God will not overrule them. Long ago, in hot Alexandria, the great Christian thinker Origen acknowledged that it did not make sense to pray for the cool of spring while enduring the heat of summer. The regular succession of the seasons is mechanical, and it will not be set aside.

Third, the picture I have been developing is that

of a world of true 'becoming'. Many forms of causality are at work, and they produce true novelty in the course of what is happening. At the height of post-Newtonian mechanical fervour, Sir Isaac's great successor Laplace had spoken of a prodigious 'calculating demon', who, by total knowledge of the properties of the bits and pieces in the present, would be able to predict the future and explain the past completely accurately. Such a Laplacean world would be a world of rearrangement, not a world of true novelty. Yet, it would also be a world of bottom-up causality only, and so our 'guess' that things are different relaxes the dead hand of Laplace's demon. We may well consider this a gain, but it poses a problem for theology.

God knows things as they really are. In a world of true becoming, therefore, will he not know them in their becomingness, that is, in their temporal succession? In other words, if the future is truly open, not just a rearrangement of the past, will not God have to know the world in time, *as it develops*? If this is the case, even God does not yet know the unformed future. This is not an imperfection in God, for the future is not yet there to be known. If this is right, then there must be an experience of time within God, in addition to his eternal nature. Such a conclusion is very controversial, but I believe it to be correct, though not all will agree with me.

The classical theological idea about God's relation to time was that he beheld all of it 'at once', looking down on the entire history of the world from above, so to speak. God did not foreknow the future, he simply knew it, for past, present, and future were all simultaneously present to him. I find this hard to accept because I don't think a world of true becoming can just be laid out timelessly in the way suggested. History unrolls, rather than just existing. We make the future; it is not up there waiting for us to arrive. Of course, I believe that God is fully prepared for the future, but I do not believe he knows beforehand exactly what the choice of a free agent, or the outcome of a free process will be.

Fourth, a scientist can pray. We can take with absolute seriousness all that science can tell us and still believe that there is room left over for our action in the world, and for God's action, too. Of course, this does not mean that prayer is just filling in a series of blank cheques given us by a heavenly Father Christmas. This is why I could not expect all those patients I prayed for simply to recover, much as I hoped they would. Prayer is not magic. It is something much more personal, for it is an interaction between humanity and God.

There still remain some problems about prayer for us to consider. The first question is, why do we have to pray at all? Why do we have to ask God for things? After all, God is good. Will he not give us what is good for us without our having continually to ask him for it? What are we doing when we pray? Are we attracting God's attention, which might otherwise be somewhere else? Are we making such a nuisance of ourselves that he really has to do something about it? Are we—and you often get this impression when listening to prayers in church—suggesting some rather cunning plan for the world's future that he might not have thought of? Obviously not. Prayer cannot be any of these things. So, what *are* we doing when we pray?

I think we are doing two things. One is as follows. I have spoken about a physical world that is supple and open to the future, a world of true becoming. We have our little part to play in bringing about this future; we have our little room for manoeuvre. God has also reserved to himself some providential room for manoeuvre in bringing about the future of the world. When we pray, the first thing we do is we offer our room for manoeuvre to be taken by God and used by him in the most effective way in relation to his room for manoeuvre, in accordance with his providential will. In more traditional language, we offer our will to be aligned with the divine will. I believe that when this alignment takes place, things become possible that are not possible when human and divine wills are at cross purposes. Therefore, prayer is genuinely instrumental. It genuinely changes the world.

An illustration I often use is one taken from science. It's the parable of laser light. What makes laser light have its unusual properties is that it is what the physicists call 'coherent'. The light is made up of waves, and, in coherent light, all the waves are in step. All the crests come together and add up to the maximum effect; all the troughs come together and add down to the maximum effect. Light that is incoherent, where the waves are out of step, has the likelihood that a crest and a trough coincide and cancel each other out. When we pray, we are seeking for a laser-like coherence between our will and God's. This has two consequences. One is that prayer is not a substitute for action, rather, it is a necessary component of action. If I have a lonely, but tiresomely repetitive elderly neighbour, I do not absolve myself of my responsibility simply by praying for the neighbour, I have to go round and listen, yet again, to the stories of youthful times. The other consequence is that it explains something that we intuitively feel is the case, but which otherwise might seem a bit puzzling. We feel that it is a good thing to have many people praying for the same cause. What is the force of this? More fists beating on the heavenly door and so more likely to attract the divine attention? I think not. However, more wills being aligned with the divine will and, therefore, greater power at work in the divine–human collaboration that is the act of petitionary prayer; this is what we are doing when we pray together.

There is another thing we are doing when we pray, and I learned this from an Oxford philosopher, John Lucas. He says that when we pray, we are called on to say what it is we really want. We are called on to commit ourselves to what it is we really value in the world. I find this a sobering and a helpful thought. In the Gospel, when the blind man comes to Jesus, the Lord says to him, 'What do you want?' It is perfectly clear what he wants, but he has to say, 'Lord that I may receive my sight' before he is healed. We are called, when we pray, to commit ourselves to what it is we really value in the world. Of course, we have to seek to pray in God's will. God takes our wishes seriously, but they do not overrule his benevolent purposes.

When we speak of prayer, we have always to

wrestle with and to recognize the very deep mysteries of the strangeness of individual destiny. There is no facile, simple account of God's providence. Often it is strange and perplexing to us in the way it works out.

I had a friend who, some years ago, was diagnosed as having terminal cancer. He was given six months to live. It was a great shock; it came out of the blue. He was a Christian, as was his wife, and they had wise Christian friends. His wife was encouraged to pray with my friend daily, and to lay her hands on him, seeking God's healing. They did so faithfully, day by day. My friend died almost exactly six months from the time that he had received the diagnosis from his physician. When he died, his wife asked herself, what had been the answer to her prayers? Only she could answer this question. Nobody could come in from the outside and tell her what God was doing in their lives. Her answer was this. Her husband, my friend, had been the centre of a lot of antagonism in his life, there were a lot of people opposed to him, but they had been deeply impressed by the fortitude and faith with which he faced his impending death. This had a very fruitful effect on the community in which he lived. Relationships were healed. He also had a condition that could have led to a very distressing death, but, actually, he had a very peaceful end in his own home. So, my friend's wife was able to conclude that her prayers *had* been answered in these ways, though, I think it's fair to say, they were not answered in the way she had been hoping for when she and her husband had first begun to pray together. Clearly, they had been hoping for more life together and for his physical recovery.

There is a mystery in individual destiny that it is part of the spiritual life to accept at the hand of the Lord. This destiny may be fulfilled by physical recovery or by accepting the imminent destiny of death. No one can say beforehand which it will be, and only those directly involved are able to interpret their own experiences. Our prayers have to have this kind of openness about them. It is the only spiritually authentic way in which a scientist, or anyone else, can pray.

6

What About Miracles?

In the last chapter I suggested that science is beginning to describe a world in which both we and God
can be understood to act. Far from history being an
inevitable mechanical process, the future is open,
and divine providence and human action play parts
in bringing it about, within the flexibilities of physical process.

So far so good, but what about miracles? Christianity can't dodge this issue, because at its heart is
the claim of the stupendous miracle of Christ's resurrection. Whatever we may say about cloudy unpredictability, we surely can't suppose that it was
through a clever exploitation of chaos theory that
Jesus was raised from the dead, never to die again.
If this happened (as I believe it did), it was a miraculous, divine act of great power.

One of our difficulties in thinking about miracles,
is that the word covers a variety of events of different kinds. The original meaning is simply something astonishing. Amazement can arise for all sorts
of reasons. One such reason could be the exercise of
normal human power, but possessed to an unusually
high degree. To take a scientific example, the ability
of some calculating prodigies to multiply together
large numbers in their heads seems miraculous to
those of us endowed with more modest calculating

skills. We are increasingly aware of the mutual influence of mind and body. The recognition of the psychosomatic character of some illnesses makes it more intelligible that there are, indeed, healing powers that some people do seem to possess. It seems to me likely that Jesus possessed such human powers to the highest degree. If this is so, we can understand some of his healing encounters as exhibiting perfectly an ability that others possess less fully. In this way, these events are miracles in the sense of provoking astonishment (and gratitude), but not in the sense of being something totally contrary to nature.

Another class of miracle stories that seems open to 'natural' explanation centre on the possibility of meaningful coincidences. Two things happen together, each perfectly ordinary in the way it comes about, but carrying significance and causing amazement because of their simultaneity. Some of the nature miracles in the Gospel are open to this sort of interpretation. An example could be the stilling of the storm. Jesus speaks words of peace to his disciples and, at the same time, the fierce squall, which has been making them anxious, blows itself out. The significance lies in the coincidence. It is perfectly possible for faith to discover the hand of God in the event, because it could well be that his providence brings about the end of the storm, in the kind of way we considered in the last chapter. Nearly everyone, I think, has had the experience of occasional, significant coincidences occurring in their lives. I believe we are right to take them seriously, but they do not necessarily imply that the course of nature has been violently interrupted to bring them about.

When all is said and done, there remain stories of events that appear to be miracles in the popular sense of something quite contrary to nature. An example would be Jesus' turning the water into wine at the wedding at Cana in Galilee (John 2.1–11). Water and wine are so distinct chemically that there is no conceivable way that one could turn naturally into the other while sitting in a stone pot. Wasn't it rather an overkill, though, to produce this transformation by miraculous power? After all, the situation was only one of mild social embarrassment. It was a pity the wine had run out, but, doubtless, they'd all had a reasonable amount to drink before it did so. At the plain, literal level, it seems a rather absurd story. Of course, we can read it at the symbolic level, and then it makes a great deal of sense, that the presence of Jesus produces a difference like that of wine to water. We're encouraged to see it this way by hints in the telling. The reference to 'six stone jars for the Jewish rites of purification' looks like a nudge to contrast the new life in Christ with the old life under the Law. So, is it just a vivid story that got put into the text as if it were an actual happening, or is it a miraculously acted parable that Jesus actually performed? Different Christians will answer differently. I personally do not think that I have to be certain of the answer to such questions in relation to every claim for miracles found in the Bible.

It seems clear what is the underlying issue. The question of miracle is not primarily scientific, but *theological*. Science simply tells us that these events are against normal expectation. We knew this at the start. Science cannot exclude the possibility that, on particular occasions, God does particular, unprecedented things. After all, he is the ordainer of the laws of nature, not someone who is subject to them. However, precisely because they are *his* laws, simply to overturn them would be for God to act against God, which is absurd. The theological question is, does it make sense to suppose that God has acted in a new way? One thing that is theologically incredible is that God is some sort of celestial conjuror, doing a turn to impress today that he didn't think of yesterday, and won't be bothered to do tomorrow. God can't be capricious. He must be utterly consistent. However, consistency is not the same as dreary uniformity. In unprecedented circumstances, God can do unexpected things. Yet there will always have to be a deep underlying consistency that makes it intelligible, for example, that God raised Jesus from the dead that first Easter Day, while, in the course of present history, our experience is that dead men stay dead. The search for this consistency is the *theological* challenge of miracle.

A simple parable drawn from science may help here. The laws of nature do not change, they are unfailingly consistent, yet the consequences of these laws can change spectacularly when one moves into a new regime. Think of heating up some water. The temperature rises steadily in a perfectly uniform way, until it reaches boiling point. Then, something happens that, if we had not observed it every day of our lives, would astonish us. The steady rise is halted and a small quantity of water turns into a large quantity of steam. Physicists call this a 'phase change'. We have moved from the liquid regime to the gaseous regime. However, the laws of nature did not change at 100°C, it is only their *consequences* that became radically different. It is a similar kind of account, with profound continuity underlying apparently discontinuous behaviour, that we must seek if we are to understand the miraculous.

The resurrection of Jesus is the test case, as it were, for this method. Let's first ask whether or not we need to take it seriously as an actual event? Couldn't it just be another vivid story, in this case intended to convey the idea that the message of Jesus continued after his death? There have certainly been people who have seen it this way. I cannot do so myself.

It is important to recognize the strangeness of Jesus' death. Most of the world's great religious leaders—Moses, Buddha, Mohammed—died in honoured old age, surrounded by their disciples. Jesus died in mid life, deserted by all those who had put their hope and trust in him. Not only was execution by crucifixion a very painful and humiliating death, it was also a death that any pious Jew must regard as a sign of God's rejection. In the Law it says that anyone hung on a tree is under the divine curse. From the dark loneliness of Calvary come the words, 'My God, my God, why have you forsaken me?' (it says something about the honesty of the writers of the Gospels that Mark and Matthew both record this terrible cry). However remarkable Jesus' words and deeds may have been, his life apparently ends in utter failure.

If this were all there was to the story, I believe we would never have heard of him. Yet we have all heard of this wandering carpenter from a peripheral province of the Roman Empire, far away and long ago, who wrote no book and who endured so miserable an end. *Something* happened to bring this about. *Something* changed the frightened and demoralized disciples of Good Friday into those who, at Pentecost, faced the authorities and confidently proclaimed that this executed man, Jesus, is God's Lord and Christ (his chosen one, who is the key to the divine purpose). This something must have been of a magnitude sufficient to bring about so astonishing a transformation.

The disciples claimed that it was the raising of Jesus from the dead. Our earliest account of this claim is given by St Paul, when he wrote to the church at Corinth:

> For I delivered to you as of first importance what I also received, that Christ died for our sins in accordance with the scriptures, that he was buried, that he was raised on the third day in accordance with the scriptures, and that he appeared to Cephas [Peter], then to the twelve. Then he appeared to more than five hundred brethren at one time, most of whom are still alive, though some have fallen asleep. Then he appeared to James, then to all the apostles. Last of all, as to one untimely born, he appeared also to me. (1 Corinthians 15.1–8).

Paul was writing in the mid fifties (the Crucifixion was either AD 30 or AD 33). When he says he told the Corinthians 'what also I received', we can take it that he is referring to instruction he received after his sensational conversion on the Damascus Road. This would have been about three years after the Crucifixion itself. So, these verses take us far back in time, and they appeal to the living testimony of those who claimed to have seen the risen Lord.

If we want accounts of what these appearances might have been like, we have to turn to the Gospels. In their present form, they were written later— between the mid sixties and the nineties—but they were based on stories that must have been preserved orally in the early Church. The material relating to the appearances is perplexing, taking very different forms in the different Gospels. Some events are located in Jerusalem, others in Galilee, so there is very little overlap between the different accounts, yet there is a common theme, unexpected and un-emphasized, that persuades me that these accounts are based on genuine reminiscences, that they are not merely pious tales. This theme is that it was difficult to recognize the risen Jesus. Mary Magdalene mistakes him for the gardener; the couple on the way to Emmaus only realize at the end who has been talking to them; only the beloved disciple recognizes who the figure on the shore of the Lake of Galilee is; in Matthew's Gospel, when Jesus appears to a crowd of disciples in Galilee, we are even told that 'some doubted' (Matthew 28.17). This strange and persistent theme would not be expected in a collection of made-up stories. There is a matter-of-factness and lack of triumphalism in the Gospel accounts of the appearances that I find persuasive.

All the Gospels also contain stories of the empty tomb, the discovery that first Easter morning that the body of Jesus was no longer there. It is incredible that it had been stolen by the disciples as an act of deceit (do men die for what they know to be a lie?), and many have seen here the strongest evidence for the Resurrection. If the authorities did not know that the tomb was inexplicably empty, why did they not nip the troublesome Jesus movement in the bud by exhibiting his mouldering body? However, one has to be careful here. It was the normal Roman custom to cast the bodies of executed felons into a common grave. Shouldn't we suppose that the same must have happened to Jesus? Aren't the Gospel tales of an identifiable tomb, later found empty, just made-up stories of a later generation?

Contemporaries certainly did not think so, for when arguments broke out between Jews and Christians, the former seem always to have accepted that there *was* an empty tomb, but they sought to explain it by claiming that it was a trick by the disciples. I also believe that there was an empty tomb. In the story, why are Joseph of Arimathea and Nicodemus mentioned? They seem to have played no conspicuous role in the early Church, so the motive for naming them must surely be that they actually did take care of Jesus' burial. In the story of the discovery of the tomb being empty, why is it women who play the principal role? In the ancient world, their testimony was not acceptable in a court of law. Once again, the obvious explanation of the honoured role assigned to them is that they actually played it. It is often said that St Paul doesn't refer to the empty tomb, but there are lots of things he doesn't mention in his letters, and this is certainly one of them. However, in the very stripped down account from his first letter to Corinth that I've quoted, he takes space to say that Jesus 'was buried'. This suggests to me that Paul knew that there was something important and significant about the burial. Paul was a Jew and no Jew would be likely to take so purely spiritual a view of things that a man could be considered alive again while his body mouldered in his tomb.

I hope I have shown in outline (there is much more detail that could be discussed) that there is evidence motivating a belief that Jesus was raised from the dead, but how we weigh this evidence will depend on whether or not the whole idea of his Resurrection makes sense. We are back with what I believe to be the central issue about miracles. Does it make sense to believe that God acted in this unprecedented and extraordinary way? Can we see a deep consistency beneath the surface surprise of the event?

I believe the answer to these questions to be a clear 'Yes' in relation to the Resurrection. It constitutes a three-fold vindication. First, it vindicates Jesus. He did not die defeated or disillusioned, beaten by the system. The darkness of Calvary was not the last word. The three-fold pattern of life, death and resurrection makes sense in a way that life and death alone would not. Second, it vindicates God. He did not abandon the one man who wholly cast himself on him and lived his life in total trust and obedience. God's steadfast love is not defeated by the wickedness or indifference of this world. Third, it vindicates the hopes of humankind. Someone once said that there is a deep human longing that the murderer should not triumph over his innocent victim. The Resurrection of Jesus shows us that this longing will find its fulfilment. This is because Christians believe that what is unique in the Resurrection of Jesus is not *that* it happened but *when* it happened. What God did for Jesus in the midst of history, he will do for all of us at the end of history. St Paul expressed this thought in his first letter to the Corinthians when he wrote, 'For as in Adam all die, so in Christ shall all be made alive' (1 Corinthians 15.22). I will have more to say about the coherence of this hope in the next chapter and I will then also explain why I think the emptiness of the tomb is so significant and important.

Miracles are only credible as acts of the faithful God if they represent new possibilities occurring because experience has entered some new regime, where the consistencies of the past must be open to enlargement in the light of the novelty of the present. This sensitivity to regime must be the answer to one of our greatest perplexities about miracles, which is not that they happen, but that they happen so infrequently in a world that seems to cry out for more vigorous divine action. C. S. Lewis once pointed out that stories of miracles cluster around what he called, 'the great ganglia of spiritual history', times when powerful movements of religious discovery are taking place. A pre-eminent era of this kind was the life of Jesus Christ.

As a Christian, I believe that God was in Christ in a special, focused way in which he has not been present in any other person. Jesus, therefore, represented the presence of a new regime in the world (this is what he meant by proclaiming that with his coming the Kingdom, that is, the rule, of God was being realized). I believe that it is a perfectly coherent and reasonable belief that this new regime should be accompanied by new phenomena, even the raising of a man from death to a glorified and everlasting life.

7

How Will
It End?

The history of the universe is the story of a gigantic tug of war. On one side is the effect of the Big Bang, driving the matter of the world apart. On the other side is the relentless pull of gravity, trying to make things come together. These two forces are very evenly balanced and we can't tell which will win in the end. If expansion prevails, the galaxies will continue to recede from each other for ever. Within each galaxy, gravity will certainly win, and great black holes will form that will eventually decay into low-grade radiation. This way, the world ends in a dying whimper. It's not a very cheerful prospect. Are things any better if gravity wins? I'm afraid not. In this case, the present expansion will one day be halted and reversed. What began with the Big Bang will end in the Big Crunch as all matter falls back into a cosmic melting pot. This way, the world ends in a bang. Either way, ultimately all is futility. It won't happen tomorrow, of course. This fate lies tens of billions of years into the future, but it's as certain as can be that humanity, and all life, will only be a transient episode in the history of the universe.

What does religion make of this? Don't these bleak predictions deny the claim that a purpose is at work in the world? Here's a challenge we've got to take on board. I believe that the death of the universe, on a time-scale of tens of billions of years, doesn't pose a problem radically different from that presented by the even more certain knowledge of our own deaths, on a time-scale of tens of years. In each case the issue is whether hope is an illusion, whether there is, after all, someone to be trusted for a destiny beyond the chilling fact of death? The scientific prediction of cosmic futility simply reminds us that a kind of evolutionary optimism—a belief that the unfolding of history must bring progress to fulfilment—is inadequate as a ground of hope. If there really is a true and lasting hope, it can only rest in the eternal being of God himself.

This was the point made by Jesus in an argument he had with the Sadducees (Mark 12.18–27). They were a group who concentrated their belief on the Law, the first five books of our Bible. They felt they couldn't find there any promise of a destiny beyond death, so they believed in a life in this world only. They tried to make their point by posing an ingenious conundrum about a woman who had been married to a succession of brothers who had died one after the other. Whose wife then would she be in the world to come? As he often did with questioners, Jesus cut through the superficial argument to the true point at issue. He took them back to Exodus, one of the books they accepted as authoritative, and reminded them that when God spoke to Moses at the burning bush, he said, 'I am the God of Abraham, and the God of Isaac, and the God of Jacob'. Jesus commented, 'He is not God of the dead, but of the living; you are quite wrong'.

The point is that if Abraham, Isaac and Jacob mattered to God once—and they certainly did—they matter to him for ever. The same is true of you and me. God does not just cast us off as discarded broken pots, thrown on to the rubbish heap of the universe when we die. Our belief in a destiny beyond our death rests in the loving faithfulness of the eternal God.

Does such a belief make sense, though? There was a time when people thought that human beings were made up of two parts, a mortal, material body that decays at death, and a detachable, immortal spiritual soul that could survive death. It was almost as if we were apprentice angels, and death was our release from this-wordly training. I've already talked a bit about mind and body and we've seen that, though they're not identical, they do seem more intimately connected with each other than this two-part scheme describes. We appear to be unities, animated bodies rather than embodied souls. This, actually, was how the ancient Hebrews thought about human nature, so, in a sense, we've simply returned to an old idea.

So, what is the soul then? It must be the 'real me'. This certainly isn't the material of my body, because that's changing all the time. I have very few atoms left from among those that were there a few years ago. Eating and drinking, wear and tear, mean that they're continually being replaced. The real me is the immensely complicated 'pattern' in which these ever-changing atoms are organized. It seems to me to be an intelligible and coherent hope that God will remember the pattern that is me and recreate it in a new environment of his choosing, by his great act of final resurrection. Christian belief in a destiny beyond death has always centred on resurrection, not survival. Christ's Resurrection is the foretaste and guarantee, within history, of our resurrection, which awaits us beyond history.

It's important to notice that we're talking of resurrection into a new world, not just resuscitation back into the old one. It's the pattern that signifies, not the matter that makes it up. The quaint ancient idea of reassembling things as they were (so that people who'd had a leg amputated sometimes had it buried beside them for convenient access at the last day) is not what's on the agenda. The Bible speaks of a new heaven and a new earth where 'death shall be no more, neither shall there be mourning nor crying nor pain any more, for the former things have passed away' (Revelation 21.4).

Where will the new 'matter' of this new world come from? I suppose that it will come from the transformed matter of this present world, for God cares for all of his creation and he must have a destiny for the universe beyond its death, just as he has a destiny for us beyond ours. This is why the empty tomb is so important. Jesus' risen body is the transmuted and glorified form of his dead body. This tells us that in Christ there is a destiny for *matter* as well as for humanity. In fact, our destinies belong together, precisely because humans are embodied beings.

Science knows that space, time, and matter all belong together. This means that in the world to come there will be 'time' as well as 'matter'. Our destiny is everlasting life, not eternity, in that special timeless sense that belongs to God alone. God is a God of process—it is the patient way in which love works—and this will be true beyond death, as it was before it. Heaven will not be boring. Its life will be the exciting and inexhaustible exploration of the riches of the divine life, made available to us more clearly than they can be in this world. The wounds of this life will be healed, its unfinished business completed, the dross we have accumulated here will there be purged away.

It is a wonderful vision, but a nagging question may well occur to you. If the new creation is going to be so wonderful, why did God bother with the old? If *that* world will be free from pain, death, and sorrow, why did he create this one instead, which seems to have so much suffering in it?

So serious a question demands an answer. It lies, I think, in recognizing that the new creation is not a second attempt by God to do rather better what he had already done the first time round in the old creation. This present world is a world allowed by God to be itself. We've seen how an evolutionary universe is theologically understood as a creation allowed to make itself. Such a world must have death as the necessary cost of life. It cannot avoid having ragged edges and blind alleys as part of the exploration of possibility that constitutes its fruitful history. Remember how it was noted earlier that the same process that allows new life to develop also permits some cells to become cancerous. The new creation is something different. That means that it

94

can work in a different way. It is theologically understood as a new world that, through Christ, has been freely integrated with the life of the Creator. This focused divine presence, which Christians associate in this world particularly with the events called sacraments, will there be present everywhere. The new creation is not a second attempt at what went before; it is the redemption and transformation of the old. Just as Jesus could not get to Easter without going through Good Friday, so creation cannot get to its sacramental destiny, without passing through this present vale of suffering.

These are deeply mysterious thoughts, but I think they are true thoughts. Two things convince me of this. One is the Resurrection of Jesus, the seed event from which the new creation has begun to grow. The other is the deep human intuition of hope, all things to the contrary notwithstanding. Remember from earlier that when a child is comforted in the night by the parental assurance 'It's all right', a statement of profound significance is being made. I said there, too, that I do not believe it to be the uttering of a loving lie, but an insight into the ultimate nature of the reality of God. It is an affirmation of the invincible divine purpose for good.

Speculative as this chapter has been, I think it is an indispensable part of coherent Christian belief to expect a destiny beyond death, for ourselves and for the universe. Rich and fruitful as this world is, I do not think that it and its history make sense if they are the only story to be told. In the end, I suppose, the best answer to our questions about the ultimate future is 'Wait and see'. I believe we can do so, confident in the faithfulness of a God who will not allow anything good to be lost.

8

Can a
Scientist Believe?

When I left the full-time practice of science and
turned my collar round to become a clergyman, my
life changed in all sorts of ways. One important
thing did not change, however, for, in both my
careers, I have been concerned with the search for
truth.

Religion is not just a technique for keeping our
spirits up, a pious anaesthetic to dull some of the
pain of real life. The central religious question is the
question of truth. Of course, religion can sustain us
in life, or at the approach of death, but it can only
do so if it is about the way things really are. Some
of the people I know who seem to me to be the
most clear-eyed and unflinching in their engagement
with reality are monks and nuns, people following
the religious life of prayerful awareness.

In the investigations of the different aspects of
experience that concern them, it seems to me that
science and religion share a common desire to learn
what is true. Neither will attain absolute certainty
in this pursuit; both will call for a belief that is
motivated but not unquestionable. Just consider
how, in fact, they set about their task.

When I started as a research student in elementary
particle physics in 1952, we believed that matter was
made out of protons, neutrons, and electrons. The

electrons have had a pretty good run for their money, and we still regard them as fundamental. However, by 1979, when I left the subject, we had reached the conclusion that protons and neutrons are themselves made up of constituents, yet more basic. These are the famous quarks and gluons that I referred to earlier.

No one has ever seen a quark, and we believe that no one ever will. They are so tightly bound to each other inside the protons and neutrons that nothing can make them break out on their own. Why, then, do I believe in these invisible quarks? It's a long story, which I'd love to tell you, but that's not really what this book is about and so I'll have to leave the detail for another occasion. In summary, it's because quarks make sense of a lot of direct physical experience, such as the patterns in which particles can be grouped, and the strange way in which projectiles, like electrons, bounce back from collisions with protons and neutrons, just as if there were some tough and tiny constituents sitting inside.

In a rather similar way, I believe in the Big Bang. Of course, I wasn't around to see it happen, but it makes sense of the way the universe appears to be today, with galaxies moving apart from each other, and with a whisper of radio noise around (the background radiation), which is best understood as a lingering echo from those far-off times.

I also believe in biological evolution. There are unresolved puzzles, some of the evidence is pretty fragmentary, and there may well be more to understand about the process than has yet been unravelled by biologists. Nevertheless, that life has grown from initial simplicity to present complexity through an evolving history, which certainly includes the patient sifting and accumulation of small differences through natural selection, is far and away the best understanding we have arrived at of the fossil record and of the relationships of DNA sequences in different organisms.

The intellectual strategy of science is neither an undue credulity *nor* a perpetual scepticism. No progress would be made if one questioned everything all the time. In fact, scientists find it as hard as anyone else to revise long-held beliefs when, occasionally, this is called for. The understanding we gain is never beyond a peradventure, and, often, there are aspects of what's going on that are puzzling or even totally inexplicable. We do the best we can, and a general scientific theory is broadly persuasive because it provides the best available explanation of a great swathe of physical experience. The cumulative fruitfulness of science encourages me to believe that this is an effective intellectual strategy to pursue.

I wish to engage in a similar strategy with regard to the unseen reality of God. His existence makes sense of many aspects of our knowledge and experience: the order and fruitfulness of the physical world; the multilayered character of reality (see page 61); the almost universal human experiences of worship and hope; the phenomenon of Jesus Christ (including his Resurrection). I do not want to elaborate these considerations here (any more than I elaborated the reasons for some of my scientific beliefs), but I think that very similar thought processes are involved in both cases. I do not believe that I shift gear in some strange intellectual way when I move from science to religion. In particular, I do not claim that religious belief springs from some mysteriously endorsed and unquestionable source of knowledge that is not open to rational assessment and, if necessary, to reassessment. Theology has long known that our images of God are inadequate to the infinite richness of his nature; that human concepts of God are ultimately idols to be broken in the face of the greater reality.

In their search for truth, science and religion are intellectual cousins under the skin. In the nineteenth century, A. D. White wrote a celebrated book called *The Warfare of Science and Theology in Christendom* (Appleton, 1896), but its thesis of conflict was a costly and ill-judged mistake. I have sought, instead, to present an account of the *friendship* between science and theology, which I believe to be the truer assessment.

Religion is our encounter with *divine* reality, just as science is our encounter with *physical* reality. A scientist *can* believe (and many do). I'm glad to count myself in that number, and I've written this book in the hope that it will help others to make a similar discovery.

Further Reading

If this book has whetted your appetite for thinking about science and religion, there are a variety of books that carry the matter further. With the shamelessness so characteristic of authors, perhaps I can mention my own writing first:

The Way the World Is (Triangle, 1983)—a defence of Christian belief at the same level as this book

One World (SPCK, 1986)—a more detailed survey of many of the issues, with quotations from other authors cited and discussed

Science and Creation (SPCK, 1988)—principally concerned with natural theology (like Chapter 2) and the Christian idea of creation (like Chapter 3)

Science and Providence (SPCK, 1989)—asks 'Does God act in the world?' and other related questions regarding prayer, miracle, and the problem of evil (like Chapters 5 and 6)

Reason and Reality (SPCK, 1991)—a more detailed discussion of particular topics, including the comparison between science and theology (like Chapters 1 and 8)

Science and Christian Belief (SPCK, 1994)—a much more detailed defence of Christian belief. One of the chapters is concerned with how the world ends (like Chapter 7) and another with combating reductionism (like Chapter 4).

Finally, if you would like to learn more about quantum theory you could try *The Quantum World* (Penguin, 1990).

For a judicious survey of the ideas of many writers in the field you could turn to Ian Barbour's *Religion in an Age of Science* (SCM Press, 1990). Biologists think about some of the issues in ways subtly different to those of physicists. In particular, they, understandably, have more to say about the significance of biological evolution. The biochemist Arthur Peacocke has written *Creation and the World of Science* (Oxford University Press, 1979) and *God and the New Biology* (Dent, 1986).

Someone concerned with questions of natural theology who approaches them from outside any religious tradition is Paul Davies. See his *God and the New Physics* (Dent, 1983) and *The Mind of God* (Simon and Schuster, 1992). An excellent book on the Anthropic Principle is John Leslie's *Universes* (Routledge, 1989). A good account of chaos theory is given in James Gleick's *Chaos* (Heinemann, 1988).

John Polkinghorne is President of Queens' College, Cambridge. He is an Anglican priest and a Fellow of the Royal Society. Until 1979 he was Professor of Mathematical Physics at Cambridge University.